LOCAL
BOUNTY

Seasonal

VEGAN RECIPES

Fort Nelson Public Library
Box 330
Fort Nelson, BC
V0C-1R0

by Devra Gartenstein

BOOK
PUBLISHING
COMPANY

Summertown, Tennessee

JUL -- 2012

Library of Congress Cataloging-in-Publication Data

Gartenstein, Devra.
   Local bounty : vegan recipes using seasonal produce / by
Devra Gartenstein.
       p.   cm.
   ISBN 978-1-57067-219-4
1. Vegan cookery.   2. Cookery (Vegetables)   I. Title.

TX837.G3225 2008
641.5'636—dc22

                                          2008025591

© 2008 Devra Gartenstein

Cover and interior design: *Aerocraft Charter Art Service*

All rights reserved. No portion of this book may be reproduced
by any means whatsoever, except for brief quotations in reviews,
without written permission from the publisher.

Printed in Canada

Book Publishing Company
P.O. Box 99
Summertown, TN 38483
888-260-8458
www.bookpubco.com

ISBN 13: 978-1-57067-219-4

17 16 15 14 13 12 11 10 09 08   1 2 3 4 5 6 7 8 9

Book Publishing Co. is a member of Green
Press Initiative. We chose to print this title on
paper with postconsumer recycled content,
processed without chlorine, which saved the
following natural resources:

68 trees

3,293 pounds of solid waste

24,956 gallons of water

5,102 pounds of greenhouse gases

48 million BTU of total energy

For more information, visit
www.greenpressinitiative.org.

*Paper calculations from Environmental Defense
Paper Calculator, www.papercalculator.org*

Contents

Introduction   1

Simplicity   5

A Brief Tour of the Vegetable Kingdom   7

Useful Techniques for Preparing Vegetables   19

Seasoning   23

Spring   25

Summer   51

Fall   101

Winter   151

Glossary   173

Index   177

For Dena—You know why

Introduction

Most Sundays during the first year that Seattle's Ballard Farmers' Market ran all winter, only one vendor showed. Judy Kirkhuff, the market manager, recalled, "Some weeks I found myself wishing they wouldn't come. But they did, week after week, because they had to pay their electric bill, or fix their car, or whatever. As long as they showed, we had a market." Anselmo's Organic Farm now occupies a corner stall at the bustling event, which was recently voted the best farmers' market in the city by readers of the *Seattle Weekly*. Even during the winter there are enough vendors to close the brick-lined Ballard Avenue to vehicle traffic.

The Pacific Northwest has one of the longest growing seasons in the country. Following Ballard's lead, several other neighborhoods now have markets that run into the winter. It takes fortitude to take part in a winter market, even in a place like Seattle, where it rarely snows. It does rain, sometimes all day, and the worse the weather, the fewer the customers. But it can be downright inspiring to see the shoppers who do turn out week after week, regardless of the conditions. They approach the winter offerings with openness and curiosity, making friends with Brussels sprouts, Savoy cabbage, turnips, and obscure varieties of kale.

As spring buds, salad greens become more abundant, and then the first asparagus appear. There are some greenhouse tomatoes as early as May, and flowers and spring onions; you'll also find herb and vegetable starts to bring home and plant in your own garden. Strawberries are the first berries, followed by raspberries, salmonberries, blueberries, huckleberries, and gooseberries. Summer squash shows up in July, sometimes earlier, sometimes later in the month, depending on the weather. Peaches and apricots make their appearance, along with tables full of cherries, some sweet, some tart. Then the tomatoes arrive in full force: green, orange, purple, red, yellow, and the remarkable tiger-striped varieties. Melons fill massive bins. Wreaths of chiles adorn the sides of tents.

Early in September, the first winter squash appear. Dimpled acorn squash stand next to smooth butternuts, and the sweet, tender delicatas take the edge off the turning of the weather. Kabocha pumpkins thicken soups, and the Cinderella varieties are so voluptuous it's hard to cut into them. By then, apple season is in full swing. Sweet, tempting samples beckon: Pink Ladies, Honey Crisps, and Cameos.

I run a concession stand at the Ballard Market, as well as several others in the Seattle area, preparing a mix of grilled vegetables, lightly seasoned, changing throughout the year. It's heavy on the greens and cabbage in the winter; yet you'd be surprised at how many kinds of greens and cabbage are available. In the spring, it's accented with asparagus, and in the summer the colorful pattypans are the highlights.

I like to feed the farmers in exchange for produce. Sometimes I choose from their offerings; other times I let them bring me whatever they have in excess, when the crops are so prolific that sales can't keep up or bad weather keeps customers away. I use a lot of what I acquire in the mix for the grill, but I also take the opportunity to experiment, coming up with ideas for fruits and vegetables that I wouldn't ordinarily serve. Many of the recipes in this book have come from these culinary adventures, efforts to synthesize whatever the vegetable gods send my way.

The marriage of vegan foods and seasonal produce is a natural one: plant-based foods follow annual cycles. A diet based on plant foods is at its best when it takes advantage of seasonal bounty and rises to the challenge of innovating during times of the year when fresh produce is scarcer and ostensibly less interesting. Like vegan eating, a diet based on seasonal foods is healthful and environmentally sustainable. Produce eaten at its prime is at its freshest—that is, at the peak of its flavor and its fullest nutritional value. Fresh foods need no chemicals; they are eaten right away, rather than preserved. Because seasonal offerings change, we eat an especially varied diet when we use them, taking in a wide range of nutrients.

We use fewer resources when we eat local foods in season. They are grown closer to home, so less fossil fuel is burned in order to bring them to the table. When I eat asparagus in May, it's usually grown in the state where I live; when I eat it in December, it's likely grown in South America. The average produce item in the typical American supermarket travels between 1,500 and 2,500 miles from the farm to the grocery shelf. A head of lettuce grown in California and shipped to Washington, DC, uses thirty-six times as much energy in transport as it provides in nutritional calories.

Local produce uses less electricity, because it doesn't need to be refrigerated during a cross-country journey. About 80 percent of the energy used in food production goes toward processes other than actually growing the food, such as shipping, storing, and refrigerating it. Locally grown produce is also more likely to be grown by a smaller outfit than a larger one: it takes a big company to ship something halfway around the world, while a smaller operation can sell its goods at a farmers' market or a roadside stand. Smaller farms tend to use fewer pesticides than larger outfits, whether or not they are certified organic. Their proprietors often handle their own produce, rather than hiring strangers, so they are inclined to minimize their contact with harmful chemicals.

I like to think that eating foods grown close to home and supporting small-scale farmers is one way of helping to create the kind of world I'd like to see. Local agriculture is an antidote to globalized industry, which wrecks long-standing traditions in Third World countries by forcing sub-sistence farmers off their land. Industrial agriculture strives for efficiency by planting vast swaths of single varieties of particular crops, opting for subspecies that ship well rather than those with the fullest flavor. This practice of monoculture creates havens for predatory insects, calling for toxic doses of pesticides. The Irish potato famine of the nineteenth century is perhaps the most devastating and lethal instance of monoculture gone awry. Because they had only planted a single subspecies of potato, a narrowly adapted bug was able to efficiently wipe out the entire country's food supply.

Today's innovative independent producers select seeds with an eye toward genetic diversity as well as food security, often reviving useful, largely forgotten heirloom plant varieties. These "radical" farmers choose fruits and vegetables for their flavor and texture, qualities that appeal to those who eat them rather than those who ship them. Planting fields with a variety of crops rather than a single kind makes them less vulnerable to pests, lessening the need for pesticides.

Growing fruits and vegetables in this manner provides meaningful work for the farmers, who could choose much easier ways to make a living. The use of little or no pesticides benefits the environment; in fact, many small-scale and organic farmers become involved in restoration projects that regenerate streams and forests, providing habitat for plants and wildlife. Farmers who live and work on their own farms tend to be connected to their communities. They are accountable to their neighbors, whom they feed and employ. And, of course, cooks and consumers take pleasure in using fresh and appealing ingredients.

A diet based on seasonal ingredients doesn't have to be a sacrifice. We've grown accustomed to having apples in May and strawberries in

December, flown in from halfway around the world, but we gain so much in flavor when we eat these foods fresh and ripe and locally grown. We also save money: unlike cars or furniture, low produce prices often correlate with high quality, because fruits and vegetables in season are abundant, and their cost isn't padded with the price of shipping.

We live in an exciting culinary time. Although we are surrounded by fast and processed foods, we have considerably more tasty, wholesome ingredients available to us than we had thirty years ago. Organic foods are the fastest growing segment of the grocery industry. (For better or for worse, even Safeway and Wal-Mart are getting in on the action.) New farmers' markets open every year. The passion for wholesome food has grown from a fringe movement to a thriving mainstream industry. In fact, fresh, seasonal produce has attained the status of gourmet or specialty food. Perhaps more than at any other time in history, the foods that are chic are actually good for us; that is, they are nutritious and beneficial for the environment, and they even taste good.

The recipes in this book are designed to give you a solid starting place for cooking with local produce, wherever you live, even if you don't have much extra time. I focus on ingredients that grow in most temperate climates: leafy greens in the spring; tomatoes, peppers, and summer squash during the summer and fall; and root vegetables and winter squash during the colder months.

Here are a few basic guidelines: When locally produced ingredients are available, try to use them. Look for opportunities to base your meals on these foods. Ask questions about where your ingredients are produced. Read labels and signs at the supermarket. Support your local farmers' market.

Simplicity

We live in an age of celebrity chefs and televised cooking competitions sporting elegant plates of expertly stacked entrées. But you don't need to create elaborate preparations or use complicated techniques in order to prepare wonderful food. The better your ingredients, the less you really need to fuss with them. There is a famous story about Alice Waters, founder of the venerable Chez Panisse restaurant in Berkeley, long-term food activist, and pioneer of the fresh, organic, local foods movement. She traveled across the country to act as a guest chef for an event featuring various eminent culinary professionals. For her contribution, she brought freshly picked heirloom salad greens and prepared a simple dressing. A fellow chef sneered, "That's not cooking, that's shopping!" And Waters responded, "Exactly."

Many cookbooks approach their recipes as secrets of the temple, which their authors impart to those brave enough to venture the necessary steps to be like them. I'm more interested in offering blueprints for wonderful meals that can be made by anyone with a little bit of background and experience, without a lot of effort. You shouldn't have to track down twenty ingredients to prepare a recipe, and making dinner needn't take up half your day. Cooking doesn't have to be stressful; in fact, if it is, the food probably won't taste as good.

In this book, I've tried to use mostly ingredients that are widely accessible and include suggestions for substitutions when feasible. If you can't make it to the farmers' market regularly, it's still worth preparing many of these recipes using store-bought ingredients. Work with what you have and add to it over time.

Shopping at farmers' markets and preparing meals from scratch take more time than buying convenience foods at mainstream supermarkets, but these activities don't have to feel like chores. Many farmers' markets include musical entertainment, activities for children, and food to eat on-site. They are community gathering places, very different from corporate superstores, where we usually want to spend as little time as possible, despite their best efforts.

The inconvenience of cooking from scratch has certainly been exaggerated for us by ads designed by companies aiming to sell us convenience products. These processed foods have much higher profit margins than the raw ingredients we buy when we cook for ourselves. It does take more time to prepare a real meal than it does to pop a frozen dinner into the microwave. But it doesn't take that long to chop some vegetables and cook them on the stovetop with some simple seasoning, while cooking a pot of rice on another burner. The more often you do it, the less time it will take. You will get more efficient as you develop routines. As you become more proficient, it will become more fun, which will make you want to do it more, which in turn will make you more proficient. Give it a try.

Cabbage

Cabbage is traditionally associated with poverty and subsistence living. Think of the stereotypical image in Russian novels of the dank hallway smelling of old cabbage. Cabbages grow well in cooler climates, and they have a fairly long shelf life. They also lend themselves to preservation by fermentation in dishes such as sauerkraut and kim chee.

Asian cabbages come in a wide variety of shapes, sizes, and shades of green. Napa cabbages are oblong and have light green curly leaves. These are best for kim chee, which traditionally needs to ferment in an earthenware crock for quite some time. You can make a quick version by tossing some chopped leaves with salt, rice vinegar, chopped garlic, and dried red chile flakes. Add a little water and put a plate on top. Then place a heavy jar on top of the plate so the cabbage will stay submerged, and keep it in the refrigerator. It will be tasty in a few hours, and even better in a few days.

Bok choy has white stems and darker green leaves. It provides both greens and substantial vegetable matter in the same plant. Baby bok choy is tender, and it's usually the best thing to buy when you are cooking in relatively small quantities. The larger bok choy tend to be too big to use all at once. Bok choy is the ideal vegetable to use in Asian stir-fries and soups. It's appealing when it's lightly cooked, and also when it's been stewed for a while. It has many close relatives that are also worth using, such as tatsoi and choy sum.

Brussels sprouts are tiny cabbages. They have something of a bad reputation, perhaps because they are so often overcooked. If you had a bad experience with them at some point, take another look at them. You can trim the bottoms and cut them in quarters, or cut a little X in the bottoms after you trim them to help them cook through to the center. Steam them and toss them with oil, vinegar, salt, and pepper, or panfry them in olive oil for a few minutes with garlic and whatever winter herb you enjoy.

Savoy cabbages are worth knowing as well: they are round, curly leaf cabbages with a delicate flavor. They are wonderful simply panfried with a little bit of seasoning and served as a side dish.

The standard green cabbage works well in salads, because it does a good job of taking on flavors when it is marinated. Coleslaw is a common food that can be very special, and you can make versions of it that go with a wide range of cuisines. Use a basic foundation of cabbage, vinegar, and vegan mayonnaise, and change the seasoning to complement whatever dish you are making. I like to add a little bit of red cabbage to my coleslaw to brighten it up. I also use thinly sliced red cabbage in green salads during the wintertime and spring, when the tomatoes aren't really worth eating.

Green cabbage works well when you braise it; that is, cook it covered, with a little bit of liquid. Use salted vegetable stock or any kind of sauce you like. You can cook it until it's just tender, or you can let it go longer if you like it very soft. Stuffed cabbage is a staple in many culinary traditions. Peel off the larger outer leaves, taking care not to rip them. Blanch them; that is, cook them in boiling water for 10 to 15 seconds to make them soft and flexible. (Find some other use for the inner part of the cabbage.) Place a spoonful or two of any kind of grain pilaf in the center of each leaf and roll them up like a burrito. Use a sauce or gravy that complements the pilaf you are using, and spread a little bit of it in the bottom of a baking dish. Arrange the rolls in the baking dish with the seams facing down, and spoon some more sauce on top. Bake them long enough to heat them through and soften them.

Really fresh green cabbage has darker green leaves on the outside. Most grocers will peel off these outer layers as the cabbage gets older and they start to wilt. The white cabbages you see in many mainstream grocery stores have had so many leaves removed that they've reached the colorless inner parts. Choose greener cabbages, if you can find them. The outer leaves are sometimes too tough to eat, but you can be certain that the insides will be very appealing.

Chiles

Before the "discovery" of the Americas, cooks in other parts of the world used black pepper to make their food spicy. Black pepper grows in a limited range of climates, so in many places it was an expensive imported item. The discovery of chiles in the Americas provided an affordable alternative for satisfying the already acquired taste for culinary heat. Chiles are widely adaptable, growing in a range of climates and exhibiting tremendous genetic variation. In fact, many parts of the world have developed unique varieties that have come to be characteristic of regional cuisines far from the plant's original home in the Americas. Paprika is an Eastern European adaptation, and superhot Thai chiles are an established ingredient in Southeast Asian dishes.

Chiles have plenty of flavor besides the heat; hence the many milder varieties. In fact, bell peppers are a variety of chile that has no heat whatsoever. I like my food spicy, but it only takes a few hot chiles to achieve a considerable amount of heat, so I often use a mixture of mild and hot ones to make the most of the chile flavor, especially when making salsa. Anaheim, pasilla, and poblano chiles tend to be relatively mild and very tasty, and there are some wonderful sweet Italian varieties. In general, smaller chiles tend to be very hot, and chiles the size of a bell pepper tend to be milder, although this is certainly not always the case. In fact, you'll find considerable variation even within a single variety: I've eaten Anaheim chiles with almost no heat at all, and others that were nearly as hot as jalapeños. Taste and experiment. Be brave.

You can roast chiles over an open flame or under the broiler in the oven until their skins are blackened. Then place them in a paper bag for a few minutes, until the condensation makes the skins soft enough to rub off. I prefer to rub some olive oil on the skins, and then roast the chiles in the oven on high heat (400 to 450 degrees F) for about 45 minutes, until they start to brown. The oil softens the skins so they don't have to be removed, and they take on a wonderful flavor from the roasting process. This isn't traditional, but it is quite tasty.

You can dice chiles, sauté them with onions and garlic, and then cook them with beans or vegetables, or both. Again, choose chiles that suit your tolerance for heat; but even if you like it hot, include mild ones as well for added flavor. You can cook chiles with whatever you are making, or if you are cooking for people with various levels of tolerance to heat, you can slice the chiles and offer them raw, on the side, as an optional garnish. Don't touch your eyes (or other sensitive body parts) after you've been handling chiles. If you wear contact lenses, it's a good idea to use gloves when you cut chiles, because the oils can stay on your hands for a while, even after you wash them.

Dried chiles are appealing as well. You can add the small Chinese ones directly to stir-fries (but be sure to warn your guests about them).

Red ancho and California chiles are medium-hot; boil them for a few minutes to soften them, and then chop or purée them. Chipotles are hotter, and they have the added advantage of their smoky flavor, which can be especially useful when you are creating vegan versions of dishes that traditionally use smoked meats. Using both fresh and dried chiles together gives extra layers of flavor to salsas and bean dishes.

Greens

In general, the tougher the greens, the longer they will take to cook. Curly leaf kale takes the longest; collards also take a while. The exact length of time depends on the temperature of the burner (the higher the heat, the less time is needed), the quantity of greens being cooked, the size of the pieces, whether or not the stems are included, how much moisture is in the pan, and, of course, your personal preference. I like to cook greens until they just start to lose their bright green color, but many people like them very, very tender, especially those who have grown up with traditional Southern food. Other people enjoy eating them raw. Some innovative farmers pick their kale when it is very young and include it in their salad mix.

One simple way to prepare greens is to steam them and season them with oil and vinegar or your favorite salad dressing. Steam curly leaf kale for at least 5 minutes. Collard greens and softer kinds of kale—the Red Russian variety with the purple vein or the wrinkly dinosaur kale (Lacinato)—take a little less time. Chard takes 2 to 3 minutes, and spinach only takes 1 to 2 minutes. Check the pot often if you are not used to cooking a particular green; that will help you to learn how long it takes for it to reach a point that you find appealing.

You can cook greens with onion and garlic, or just garlic. If you are using onion, heat it in olive oil until it's translucent; if you are just using garlic, cook it for less than a minute, just until you can smell it. You'll need enough oil to coat the onion and garlic, but you don't have to coat the greens with oil. Sprinkle in some salt when you add the greens: it helps draw out the moisture in them and speeds up the cooking process. You can also drizzle in a little bit of water when you add the greens. It steams them, which helps them to cook faster. Use enough water to create steam, but not enough to collect on the bottom of the pan. If you are working with a lot of greens, you can still fit them in a relatively small pan by cooking a few handfuls at a time, then adding more when they cook down, mixing as you go.

Some people prefer their greens with the stems removed; others like to eat the whole plant. Again, experiment and learn what appeals to you. Personally, I enjoy the chewiness of collard stems, but kale ribs are too tough for me. Younger plants have more tender stems (and leaves). Chard ribs aren't particularly tough, and they can be quite visually appealing, especially the red, pink, orange, and yellow rainbow chard. Taste the stems and decide for yourself whether you want to include them.

Fresh Herbs

Before the invention of high-speed transportation, ships sailed from the Middle East and Europe to Southeast Asia on journeys that could take months, carrying precious cargoes of cloves, cinnamon, ginger, nutmeg, and pepper. The prices commanded by these spices were so high that nations fought wars over trade routes. The quest for these aromatics fueled the frenzied exploration of the globe during the fifteenth and sixteenth centuries, which led to the "discovery" of the Americas. Fresh herbs, which grow abundantly in temperate climates, were not valued in the same way. Nowadays, we hear cooking experts telling us not to keep spices on our shelves for longer than a few months, because they grow stale. If this is the case, then the coveted products arriving in Europe on ships from the East five hundred years ago weren't even of particularly good quality. They spent more time in transit than we are supposed to keep them in our pantries.

Today, even middle- and low-income households stock their shelves with an array of spices, but, with the exception of a few common varieties, such as parsley and cilantro, fresh herbs have become something of an indulgence. Unlike the spices that scented affluent medieval tables, fresh herbs don't really have to be luxury items, although they certainly are special. It only takes a bit of time and initiative to grow them yourself. Bunches available at farmers' markets are larger and more affordable than those in grocery stores. For the moderate time or expense they ask of us, they offer dimensions of flavor well worth having.

Basil is the star of Italian meals, especially when you use it with its best friend, the tomato. You can use it either raw or cooked, but if you are cooking it, add it near the end of the cooking time so its flavor will stand out. Thai basil has reddish stems and pointier leaves, and it tastes almost minty. It fits in well with Southeast Asian dishes. Use it with fresh mint and cilantro, or with coconut milk and lime. With both kinds of basil, leaves that haven't yet flowered are best; but if you do find flowers, you should remove them.

Use cilantro in Mexican, Indian, or Southeast Asian dishes. Of all the herbs I know, it's the one that people tend to dislike the most. But even people who think they dislike it often don't mind it when it's cooked with other foods, or even when it is used with restraint along with other ingredients that complement it well, such as tomatoes and chiles. There are also many people who love it, undisguised and even prominent. Decide for yourself how you feel about it and how you want to use it.

Fresh dill is one of my favorite seasonings, probably because my grandmother used it so often. It works well in Greek and Eastern European dishes and is equally good in summer salads like potato salad and coleslaw. It's also ideal for quick pickles, such as those made with beets or green beans.

Fresh parsley will perk up virtually any European or Middle Eastern dish. It goes well with Eastern European, French, Greek, Israeli, Italian, Lebanese, and even North African foods, among others, but avoid using it in Chinese, Indian, or Thai dishes. It is common and affordable enough to use regularly, and, in my humble opinion, you can't use too much of it. It works well either cooked or raw, especially in salads.

Rosemary is more of a winter herb, and it goes with hearty meals and stews. It especially shines with potatoes. Make sure to chop the leaves well, because they can be tough. It's better to chop rosemary by hand than in a food processor, where the bigger leaves stick to the sides. Fresh oregano and thyme can really amplify a dish, but be sure to add them sparingly, because they dominate other flavors.

The Onion Family

I think of the members of the onion family as fine supporting actors. They add depth and nuance to whatever you are cooking, without needing to claim center stage. Like bass notes in music, their flavors often contribute to a dish in ways that don't stand out enough to be specifically identified, yet the total effect would certainly seem less complete if they were missing. Besides the standard onion, the common members of this family include chives, garlic, green onions (scallions), leeks, and shallots.

When I'm working with winter vegetables—cabbage, greens, potatoes, squash, turnips, and so forth—I like to use several members of the onion family together. Garlic, leeks, and shallots make an especially lovely combination. I tend to use them less when I'm working with summer produce, but you can use chives, green onions, and red onions raw in salads. Chives are the most innocuous member of the onion family; an oniony herb, really. Avoid using raw onions when preparing food for timid eaters. If you are including raw garlic in a dip or a salad, use very little. A small amount goes a long way, and garlic breath can be embarrassing for people in social situations, especially in formal settings.

If you are cooking garlic along with onions, leeks, and/or shallots, you can start them all together without worrying about burning them, provided you are paying attention. If you are heating garlic on its own, be very careful not to let it brown, unless you are preparing an East Asian dish. If you are cooking something else and you accidentally brown the garlic, I recommend tossing it and starting all over again; browned garlic has a strong flavor that usually doesn't fit well with most dishes.

Cook garlic, leeks, onions, and shallots in enough oil to coat them. The oil brings them to a high temperature, which releases their flavor. Once you add other ingredients, you can use liquids, such as soy sauce, vegetable stock, wine, or the moisture from tomatoes, to keep foods from sticking to the pan and burning. Cook onions and shallots until they are translucent and leeks until they are soft.

Clean leeks well by slitting them down the middle lengthwise, then washing thoroughly between the layers, especially the darker green part; they tend to have a lot of dirt in there. Some garlic bulbs have big cloves that are easy to peel; others have small, difficult-to-peel cloves that make you want to rip your hair out. Pay attention to where you buy your garlic. There are many different varieties, and even if you don't know them by name, you will start to notice which stores and which farmers carry varieties that are easy to handle.

Potatoes

These earthy tubers have been a vital part of cuisines around the world for hundreds of years, despite their reputation as peasant food—filling, but lacking in nutrients. The recent prejudice against them, spread largely by advocates of low-carbohydrate diets, is nothing new. In fact, potatoes were a tough sell in Europe when explorers first brought them over from the Americas. The governments of various European nations recognized the potential of this cool-weather crop to efficiently feed their populations, but the people themselves were suspicious. Rich people weren't eating them, so why were they trying to force them on the poor?

In France, a clever public official named Parmentier tricked the peasantry into growing potatoes by planting them in a gated garden patrolled by armed guards, ostensibly for consumption by the royal family. Then he began leaving them unguarded, so people stole them and planted them in their own gardens, as Parmentier had hoped. Potatoes did not become popular in England until street vendors began to deep-fry them. Today, we have countless varieties of potatoes available to us, from humble russets to lovely purple spuds. We know them as both a comfort food and a tasty, versatile ingredient.

Small potatoes tend to be more special than large ones. They are considerably more expensive, because they take as much land to grow as the large ones, per potato, but they yield less food. There's something really appealing about biting into these small, self-contained units. Some stores and farmers sell mixes of different colors and varieties of baby potatoes, about the size of acorns. I like to boil these—they only take about 5 minutes—and then toss them with olive oil, salt, pepper, and parsley or dill or chives.

Roasting potatoes really brings out their flavor and creates a nice, chewy exterior. It's good to parboil them before roasting them; that is, boil them for 1 to 2 minutes, not quite until they are soft, but long enough to get a head start. Toss them with olive oil and a simple seasoning, and roast them in the oven at 400 to 450 degrees F until they start to brown. You can get away with using less oil if you work it into the potatoes with your hands instead of stirring the potatoes and oil together with a utensil. Needless to say, wait until they are cool enough to handle if you are doing it this way.

If you are including potatoes in any kind of stovetop dish, it's a good idea to steam or boil them a bit before adding them to the other ingredients. Otherwise, they just take too long to cook, and you'll run the risk of overcooking the other ingredients. In soups, they can act as a thickener; cook them long enough for them to start to break down. In many culinary traditions, it's standard to peel potatoes, but there are plenty of nutrients in the skins. Go with your personal preference.

Purple potatoes taste a lot like the white ones, but they add color. I like to use them along with other varieties. Russets are the best for baking, but they get mealy if you boil them. Yukon Golds are especially tasty, as are fingerlings and butterballs. Some farmers' market vendors sell only potatoes. Get to know these growers if you love potatoes, and don't be shy about asking them about their favorites.

Squash

Summer squash include zucchini, yellow crooknecks, and the many varieties of pattypans, among others. They can be eaten raw or cooked. Winter squash appear in early fall and include acorn, butternut, delicata,

Hubbard, and spaghetti squash, as well as pumpkins. These have a long shelf life, and they do need to be cooked. I've heard that every part of the squash is edible, though I've never tried to eat the stems. Although we tend to peel winter squash, you can eat the skin if you really want to. The seeds from winter squash are wonderful roasted, and you can eat squash blossoms in salads or cooked with chiles.

Summer squash offer more in the way of color and texture than they do in flavor. I like to prepare them in ways that show off their best qualities. Use a range of colors, and be careful not to overcook them, because that will compromise both their color and texture. They are probably my least favorite vegetable to use in soups and stews, because they break down and get mushy. They are lovely raw, which makes them ideal to serve with dips or use in salads. You can also stuff them, especially the baby pattypans and sunburst squash. Blanch them for less than a minute; then scoop some pulp out of the top half and stuff them with any kind of grain pilaf. These make a great appetizer.

Delicatas are an early winter squash and also the first to disappear as the season progresses, so get them while you can. As their name suggests, they are delicate, sweet, and tender. Cut them in half lengthwise, remove the seeds, brush them with olive oil, sprinkle them with salt and pepper, and roast them at 400 to 450 degrees F for 20 to 30 minutes, or until they are fork-tender. You can roast just about any winter squash, but the delicatas especially shine this way, and they cook quickly, in about the amount of time it takes to prepare a pot of rice. If you are roasting big pieces of squash, put some water in the bottom of the baking pan to keep them from getting too dry.

You can also cook almost any kind of winter squash by peeling it and cutting it into chunks, tossing the chunks with oil and seasoning, and roasting them in the oven at high heat (400 to 450 degrees F) until they are soft, about 45 to 60 minutes. The smaller the pieces, the more quickly they will cook. If you are preparing squash this way, choose a variety with a smooth skin—really, anything other than acorn will work—and peel it with a good vegetable peeler. You can also stir-fry the chunks with other vegetables. Add the pieces to the mix early on, along with the harder root vegetables.

The pulp from winter squash makes a good binder in vegan casseroles; it's a tasty replacement for eggs. Cut the squash in half, or into quarters or eighths if it's a bigger pumpkin, and roast it in the oven or steam it on the stovetop (roasting will take longer than steaming). Either way, once it's soft, scoop out the pulp and mash it a bit. Then mix it with cooked beans, grains, and vegetables, and add your favorite seasonings. Transfer the mixture to a casserole dish, sprinkle some crunchy nuts or seeds on top, and bake it until it's heated through and starts to set.

Winter squash makes a great thickener for soups. You can steam or roast it separately; then purée it with some vegetable stock in a blender or food processor before adding it to the soup. You can also peel it, cut it into bite-size chunks, and add the pieces directly to the pot. After 30 to 40 minutes the pieces will start to break down, giving the soup some body, while also leaving some pieces intact and recognizable. Don't use spaghetti squash this way: it's too stringy and watery. In fact, avoid it in almost any recipe, unless you are taking advantage of its namesake qualities and using it as a spaghetti substitute.

Tomatoes

Nowhere is the difference between industrial produce and fresh, farm-raised vegetables more apparent than with tomatoes. There is no comparison between a hard, cold Roma tomato purchased at a mainstream supermarket in the dead of winter and a fresh heirloom tomato eaten at room temperature on the day it is picked. I have friends who refuse to eat tomatoes out of season; I don't go to such lengths myself, but I do make a point to enjoy the best summertime offerings to their fullest.

Supermarket tomatoes have, in fact, improved considerably during the past ten or fifteen years. In addition to the sturdy Romas and the generic slicing varieties, we now have hothouse tomatoes sold on the vine. One celebrity chef puts his name on some respectable, overpackaged, widely distributed tomatoes. Part of me is glad that these are available, that we've collectively reached a point where even off-season produce is of a higher quality than it was twenty years ago. But there is no substitute for a perfectly ripe tomato at the right time of year.

I'm a big fan of the beefsteak tomato. They are hybrids; that is, they were bred by crossing strains with desirable traits to produce an arguably artificial result. But this result happens to be so tasty that it's hard to quarrel with it. I know organic farmers who grow beefsteaks almost exclusively, and others who grow an impressive mix of tomatoes. I love tasting an assortment, but I find myself mostly falling back on the familiar beefsteak. My other favorite is the Sun Gold, a yellow cherry tomato that's full of flavor.

Overripe tomatoes are best for sauces. They have lots of flavor, and they are very juicy. It's okay if they are a little bruised if they are going to be cooked. In fact, you could look at the bruising as a positive trait: they bruise because they are so delicate, and they are delicate because they are at the perfect point to eat them. You can make a very quick tomato sauce by cooking some garlic in olive oil for 1 to 2 minutes, adding a couple of chopped ripe tomatoes, and cooking them on medium-high heat for the amount of time it takes a pot of pasta to cook. Season the tomatoes with salt, pepper, and fresh basil. I don't generally use dried basil in this kind of quick sauce, because it doesn't have enough time to become really flavorful.

You can use tomatoes in all kinds of salads. If you are using them when they are perfectly ripe, you really don't need anything other than oil, vinegar (balsamic is best), salt, and pepper, but fresh parsley or basil never hurts. When tomatoes are really ripe, they lose juice quickly when they are salted, so it's best to dress them right before you are going to eat them. Tomato salads are the best way to show off colorful heirloom tomatoes.

You can roast tomatoes in the oven on high heat (between 400 and 450 degrees F) for 30 to 40 minutes, until they start to brown. This makes them especially flavorful. The skins will start to peel when you do this, and you can remove them if you are so inclined, but I enjoy their caramelized flavor. You can purée roasted tomatoes for salsas or Italian tomato sauces, or you can squeeze them right into whatever you are making. Include the juice that collects on the bottom of the baking pan; it would be a shame to waste this tasty liquid. Another good use for tomatoes is to add them to stovetop mixed-vegetable dishes; they will contribute both some liquid and flavor. Put them in after the onions and garlic, or at whatever point the mixture starts to seem dry.

Braising

Braising is the practice of cooking foods tightly covered with a little bit of liquid. It differs from sautéing, which uses less liquid in the pan, and from stewing, which uses more. Like steaming, braising cooks vegetables relatively quickly, making them quite tender, but it has the added advantage of making them flavorful. While stewing is a technique generally used with a mix of foods, combining different types of ingredients such as beans and vegetables, braising is often used for side dishes that highlight a single item.

Braising works well for vegetables that absorb flavors well, and those that hold up when they are cooked until they are very tender. Don't use it for summer squash or bell peppers, because they lose their appeal when they are overcooked. Cabbage works well, as do the hardier greens such as kale and collards. Root vegetables are good candidates, as are broccoli and green beans. For your braising liquid, use a flavorful vegetable stock along with some fresh herbs, or you can dilute your favorite marinade with a little bit of water. Serve braised vegetables with rice, barley, or quinoa, and top the grains with some of the braising liquid.

Roasting and Grilling

In his seminal essay "The Culinary Triangle," French anthropologist Claude Lévi-Strauss describes the cross-cultural significance of roasted meals, as opposed to those that are stewed or fermented. He points out that roasting is generally the province of men, while women are more likely to prepare stewed meals. In a wide variety of places, hosts serve roasted foods to guests and stewed meals to their families. Roasted food speaks of celebration, of events that are not everyday occurrences. Lévi-Strauss's observations apply to a striking number of cultures in very different parts of the world. They seem to be as true of ancient Greece, where Homer described warriors roasting meat after a battle, as they are today, when barbecuing tends to be the province of men. I've personally observed that, as a caterer and restaurateur, if I use the adjective "roasted" in front of any menu item, it automatically sounds special. If Lévi-Strauss is right, our response to roasting is deep and ancient, even primeval.

When contemporary cookbooks provide instructions for roasting, they are referring to cooking foods in the oven on high heat. Although Lévi-Strauss writes about the long history of roasted foods, the technique that now goes by that name was not widely practiced until relatively recently. Most households did not have ovens until the past hundred years or so. The traditional practice of roasting is most like the modern practice of grilling, or barbecuing. It involves searing foods by cooking them over an open fire. There is a wildness about preparing food this way, even when we do it on our backyard patios.

Both grilling and oven roasting cook the moisture out of foods, concentrating their flavors and caramelizing them. In a sense, this is an inefficient way to cook: you end up with less than you had when you started. It's not the best use of resources if you are trying to feed a crowd on a limited budget, but perhaps that's part of what makes it special. Although roasting and grilling have traditionally been techniques used for meat, they also work well for vegetables, provided you marinate them or toss them in a tasty sauce to coat them before you cook them. Whatever you use to marinate your vegetables, it should have some kind of oil or some kind of sugar or fruit juice, because these ingredients will cause the food to brown. You can set aside some of the sauce to serve on the side once the food is cooked.

If you are roasting vegetables in the oven, spread them in a thin layer on an oiled baking sheet. If they are too close together, or piled on top of each other, they won't brown as nicely. If you are cooking on the grill, use slices that are thin enough to cook in the center, but thick enough that they won't break apart. You can arrange bite-size pieces on skewers, but make sure to soak the skewers in water first, so they don't catch on fire. You can also use skewers for roasting in the oven, if you are making finger food.

Zucchini lends itself nicely to either grilling or roasting, as do bell peppers, fennel, mushrooms, and onions. Eggplant also works well, especially prepared on its own, in rounds about one-quarter to one-third inch thick. If you are roasting or grilling potatoes, parboil them first by cooking them for just 1 to 2 minutes to give them a head start. Harder root vegetables such as beets, carrots, parsnips, and turnips can be quite tasty when they are roasted, but be sure to cut them into relatively small pieces so they will cook all the way through. The same is true for yams and winter squash. Don't even try to grill or roast cabbage and greens, as they will burn before they get tender.

Sautéing

Cooking food on the stovetop in a little bit of oil is a good way to release flavors, especially if you are working with the onion family, which also includes garlic, leeks, and shallots. Not long ago, many health and diet experts recommended that we eat foods low in fat, without distinguishing between harmful fats and more healthful ones. During the past few years, even mainstream studies have made a distinction between good fats and bad ones, warning against the dangers of animal fats and artificial trans fats, while touting the health benefits of olive oil and omega-3 fatty acids.

I almost always sauté vegetables in olive oil, although I don't think it's necessary to use fine extra-virgin oil for this purpose. In fact, I think that using really fine olive oil for sautéing is something of a waste of an expensive product that's better used in recipes where you can really taste it. Some people feel very strongly that one should only use the finest, freshest oils; if that's your position, then that's certainly what you should use. I tend to look for a sensible middle ground, seeking the best possible balance of health, cost, and flavor.

Once the onions and garlic are cooked, you can add a little liquid to the vegetables you are sautéing. It's best to use something that will contribute flavor, such as soy sauce or wine; you could even add a tomato, which will break down and provide some moisture. You can sauté vegetables on medium-low heat, if you are preparing a number of menu items at once and can't give them all your full attention, or you can use medium-high heat, if you are stirring often. A sautéed vegetable dish is different from a stir-fry, which you cook quickly on high heat, using an oil like canola, peanut, or safflower, with a higher smoke point than olive oil.

After the onions and garlic, add the denser, harder vegetables first, such as carrots or turnips. Eggplant is soft, but it should also be added early on, because it needs to cook for a while. Collard greens and kale can take as long as the root vegetables, but chard and spinach should be added toward the end. You can add mushrooms at any point; they provide some liquid, and it's hard to overcook them. Summer squash should go in last.

If you are cooking in quantity, you can steam some of the vegetables before adding them to the mix. It's hard to fully cook a large quantity of vegetables by just sautéing them. Even if you are using a big pan, they can't all be in contact with its surface. Always sauté the onion and garlic, and make sure there's enough seasoning to flavor the steamed vegetables you are going to add: the part you are actually sautéing may taste salty and overseasoned on its own, but once you add the steamed ingredients it will be more balanced. Taste it and adjust the seasonings.

Steaming

Steaming is the quickest and most energy-efficient way to prepare most vegetables. Unlike boiling, which leaches nutrients, steaming preserves them. If you don't have a perforated pot specifically designed for steaming, you can get an inexpensive steamer basket at most supermarkets that will work in a wide variety of pots. In a pinch, you can even place a metal colander over a little bit of boiling water and cover it.

Steamed vegetables are naturally low in fat, because they are cooked only with water. You can toss them with a little olive oil once they are done; this will impart the flavor and mouthfeel of food cooked in oil, but doesn't use nearly as much fat. I often steam vegetables separately when I'm including them in other dishes, especially root vegetables, which can take a long time to cook. If you are preparing them this way, remove them from the heat before they are fully done, because they'll cook further once you add them to the other ingredients.

As with any other cooking technique, the smaller the pieces, the quicker they'll cook. Most vegetables only need to be steamed for a few minutes if they are cut into bite-size pieces. Cook green vegetables until they are bright green, but turn off the heat before they begin to lose their color. If you are steaming food that you are not going to serve right away, it's a good idea to undercook it a bit. It will continue to cook while it sits, even if there's no heat under it.

Seasoning

Foods from different parts of the world take their distinctive flavors from traditional combinations of seasonings. By familiarizing yourself with these combinations, you can improvise and create convincing regional dishes. Our relationship with food is deeply emotional: we enjoy the meals we do in part because they evoke memories—conscious or otherwise—of foods we have enjoyed in the past, the people who have shared them with us, and the occasions they have marked. By staying true to traditional seasonings, we are able to stir memories and create comfort foods. This is especially important when preparing vegan meals for those who are not used to eating this way. The very absence of meat and dairy may put them in unfamiliar territory, and the use of familiar seasonings can help bring them back into their comfort zone.

Perhaps traditional seasoning combinations work because we are used to tasting certain flavors together. It is also likely that some combinations naturally blend, such as herbs that share a common ancestry, genetically speaking. Whatever the cause, traditional flavor combinations have much in common with musical scales, where certain sequences of notes naturally sound right together. Musical conventions may vary dramatically from one part of the world to another, but we recognize the patterns of the music we have heard over time, and we find them satisfying.

This is not to say that we should never play with flavors, blending seasonings in unconventional ways. But we do a better job of tweaking conventions when we know just what it is we are leaving behind. Here are some traditional seasoning combinations that can provide a working foundation. This list is very general and by no means comprehensive. There are countless regional variations, and, of course, I have focused on the areas that I know best. I have also simplified, for the sake of creating a relatively concise list. You can combine any or all of the seasonings I've listed together on a single line. Combinations that I've listed on separate lines don't necessarily go together, but can be used alternately to create the flavors of a regional cuisine.

AFGHAN	■ dill, cardamom, cilantro, cumin, mint
CAJUN	■ bottled hot sauce, liquid smoke, Worcestershire sauce (there are vegan options)
CHINESE	■ rice vinegar, soy sauce, toasted sesame oil
EASTERN EUROPEAN	■ caraway, dill, paprika
GREEK	■ anise, dill, lemon ■ dill, lemon, oregano ■ cinnamon, lemon, tomato
INDIAN	■ cardamom, coriander, cumin, ginger, turmeric
ITALIAN	■ basil, garlic, oregano
JAMAICAN	■ allspice, coconut milk, thyme
JAPANESE	■ rice vinegar, soy sauce, sugar
MEXICAN	■ chili powder, cumin, oregano
MIDDLE EASTERN	■ cumin, lemon, mint, parsley
THAI	■ coconut milk, lime juice, soy sauce (as a substitute for fish sauce), Thai basil

Spring

Spring is the start of the agricultural year, a time of new beginnings. It starts off lean, as we tide ourselves over with the last of the winter's offerings. By the end of the season, things start to speed up, building toward the most fruitful parts of the year. Spring gives us the opportunity to enjoy the early, tender stages of many vegetables' life cycles: kale buds, baby beets, spring onions, young garlic, and baby carrots. We also have the classic spring produce: asparagus, morel mushrooms, strawberries, and sugar snap peas. It is a time of hope and anticipation, when each new item heralds the bountiful time ahead.

Spring Produce

EARLY SPRING	MID-SPRING	LATE SPRING
carrots	asparagus	snow peas
kale buds	baby beets	strawberries
leeks	garlic scapes (stems)	sugar snap peas
radishes	lettuce	
sorrel	morel mushrooms	
spring onions	parsley	
young garlic	pea vines	
	sea beans (salicornia)	
	spinach	
	thyme	

Morel Mushroom Gravy

Morel mushrooms appear in the spring in most parts of the country. Their flavor is deep and earthy, adding an unusual twist to a traditional gravy. Unless you know something about hunting mushrooms—or you are working under the tutelage of someone wise and experienced—do not try gathering your own. There are poisonous varieties out there, and the risk is too great. Foragers sell them at farmers' markets, and during the right time of year you can also find them in some conventional stores.

2 tablespoons olive oil

½ onion, chopped

6 to 8 morel mushrooms, sliced

1 teaspoon dried basil

½ teaspoon dried thyme

½ teaspoon salt

3 tablespoons unbleached white or whole wheat flour

1 cup water

1 teaspoon vegan Worcestershire sauce

1. Heat the oil in a small saucepan. Add the onion, mushrooms, basil, thyme, and salt. Cook on medium-low heat for about 5 minutes, until the onion is translucent and the mushrooms begin to release their juice.

2. Add the flour and mix well.

3. Stir in the water and Worcestershire sauce and mix well. Slowly bring the mixture to a boil, stirring often. When the gravy starts to thicken, lower the heat and cook for about 30 seconds longer, stirring constantly.

Roasted Garlic and Herb Sauce

YIELD: ABOUT 1 CUP

You can use this versatile sauce with pasta, or you can take a loaf of wonderful bread, cut it in half horizontally, spread some of the sauce over the cut portions, put the halves back together, wrap the bread in foil, and heat it in the oven for 15 to 20 minutes.

6 cloves garlic, unpeeled

2 tablespoons olive oil

1 cup chopped parsley

2 to 3 tablespoons fresh sage

2 to 3 tablespoons fresh oregano

½ teaspoon salt

Freshly ground black pepper

1. Preheat the oven to 400 degrees F.

2. Rub the garlic cloves with enough of the oil to coat them. Wrap them in foil and roast them in the oven for 25 to 35 minutes, or until they are soft enough that you can squeeze the pulp out of the skins.

3. When the garlic cloves are cool enough to handle, squeeze out the pulp into a food processor or blender. Add the remaining oil along with the parsley, sage, oregano, salt, and pepper to taste and process until smooth.

Roasted Leek and Carrot Soup

YIELD: 6 SERVINGS

In this recipe the roasting process concentrates the flavors and makes an exquisite broth. Use small, sweet spring carrots if you can find them.

1 pound carrots
1 pound leeks
1 medium onion
1 bulb garlic
2 to 3 tablespoons olive oil
2 quarts unsalted vegetable stock or water
1 cup white wine or a nonalcoholic substitute
1 cup chopped fresh parsley
¼ cup nutritional yeast flakes
1 teaspoon salt
2 to 3 tablespoons balsamic vinegar

1. Preheat the oven to 450 degrees F.
2. If you are using small carrots, trim the ends; if you are using big ones, trim them (peeling is optional) and cut them into 2-inch chunks. Cut the leeks in half lengthwise, clean them well, and cut them into 2-inch lengths. Peel the onion, cut it into quarters, and separate the layers. Separate the garlic into cloves, but don't peel them. Toss all of the vegetables with the oil and spread them on a baking sheet, keeping the garlic in a separate corner. Roast the vegetables for 30 to 40 minutes, or until they start to brown.
3. Meanwhile, combine the stock, wine, parsley, nutritional yeast, and salt in a medium soup pot and begin heating it on medium-low heat. When the vegetables are done roasting, squeeze the pulp out of the garlic cloves and add it to the stock along with the carrots, leeks, and onion. Simmer for about 1 hour. Remove from the heat and stir in the balsamic vinegar.
4. Strain the soup and set aside the stock. Blend the vegetables in batches in a food processor or blender, adding some of the stock, as needed, to facilitate processing. Stir the blended vegetables into the remaining stock in the pot. Taste and add additional salt, if needed. Reheat, if necessary, and serve.

West African Peanut Soup

YIELD: 4 SERVINGS

Of all the soups that we serve in my restaurant, this one is by far the most popular.

6 cups unsalted vegetable stock or water

1 medium onion, chopped

2 tablespoons peeled and grated fresh ginger

4 cloves garlic, minced

1 teaspoon salt

1 bunch collard greens (4 to 6 leaves), cut into 1-inch strips

1 cup unsalted peanut butter (chunky or smooth)

½ cup unsalted tomato paste, or 1 cup canned crushed tomatoes

Bottled hot sauce

1. Bring the stock to a boil in a medium soup pot. Add the onion, ginger, garlic, and salt. Cook on medium-low heat for about 20 minutes.

2. Add the collard greens and cook for 10 to 15 minutes longer.

3. Take 1 to 2 cups of stock out of the pot and whisk it together with the peanut butter and the tomato paste. (If you are using crushed tomatoes, you can add them directly to the pot.) Stir the peanut butter mixture into the soup and mix well.

4. Season the soup with hot sauce to taste. Simmer for 10 to 15 minutes on medium-low heat, stirring often.

Puréed Asparagus and Potato Soup

YIELD: 6 SERVINGS

The flavor of the asparagus in this recipe is subtle, but it adds a lovely dimension to a hearty soup.

2 quarts unsalted vegetable stock or water

4 medium potatoes (any kind but russets), quartered

1 bunch asparagus (about 1 pound), trimmed and cut into 2-inch pieces

1 leek, cut in half lengthwise, cleaned well, and cut into 2-inch pieces

1 parsnip, peeled, trimmed, and cut into 1-inch pieces

1 tablespoon fresh thyme

4 cloves garlic, peeled

1 teaspoon salt

Freshly ground black pepper

Juice of 1 lemon

1. Bring the stock to a boil in a medium soup pot. Add the potatoes, asparagus, leek, parsnip, thyme, garlic, salt, and pepper to taste.

2. Bring the mixture back to a boil and cook on medium-low heat for 30 minutes.

3. Strain the vegetables and set aside the stock. Blend the vegetables in batches in a food processor or blender, adding some of the stock, as needed, to facilitate processing.

4. Stir the blended vegetables into the remaining stock in the pot and add the lemon juice. Taste and add additional salt, if needed. Reheat, if necessary, and serve.

Spinach-Lentil Soup

YIELD: 6 SERVINGS

Here's a hearty soup for those chillier spring days

  6 cups unsalted vegetable stock or water

  1½ cups dried lentils

  1 medium onion, chopped

  4 cloves garlic, minced

  1 teaspoon salt

  1 tablespoon dried dill weed

  1 tablespoon chopped fresh spearmint, or 1 teaspoon dried

  4 cups chopped fresh spinach

  Juice of 1 lemon

1. Bring the stock to a boil in a medium soup pot. Add the lentils, onion, garlic, and salt. Bring the mixture back to a boil and cook on medium-low heat for about 20 minutes.

2. Stir in the dill weed and spearmint and cook for 10 to 15 minutes, or until the lentils start to break down.

3. Add the spinach and cook for 5 minutes longer.

4. Stir in the lemon juice. Taste and add additional salt, if needed, and serve.

Beet Greens with Young Garlic

In the spring, some farmers sell immature garlic that looks just like green onions but tastes and smells garlicky. The beet greens for sale during this time of year often have tiny beets attached. They cook in about the same amount of time as the greens.

2 tablespoons olive oil

3 stalks young garlic, cut into ½-inch pieces

½ teaspoon salt

1 bunch beet greens (about ½ pound) including the baby beets, chopped

1 to 2 teaspoons vegan Worcestershire sauce

1. Heat the olive oil in a medium saucepan. Add the garlic stalks and salt. Cook for about 5 minutes on medium-low heat.

2. Add the beet greens and Worcestershire sauce and cook for about 5 minutes longer, until they are tender.

Roasted Baby Carrots
with Fresh Thyme

YIELD: 4 SERVINGS

This recipe is best if you use very small (and very sweet) carrots.

2 bunches baby carrots (about 1 pound)
2 to 3 tablespoons olive oil
1 teaspoon chopped fresh thyme
½ teaspoon salt

1. Preheat the oven to 400 degrees F.
2. Trim the tops and bottoms from the carrots.
3. Toss the carrots with the remaining ingredients (you can use your hands) and arrange them on a baking sheet.
4. Roast the carrots in the oven for 35 to 45 minutes, or until they are tender and have started to brown.

Asparagus with Mustard-Dill Sauce

YIELD: 4 SERVINGS

I think about this recipe all winter, as I look forward to spring. It only takes ten minutes to prepare.

1 quart water

1 pound asparagus, trimmed and cut into 2-inch lengths

1 to 2 tablespoons olive oil

2 to 3 cloves garlic, minced

Juice of ½ lemon

1 tablespoon chopped fresh dill

1 teaspoon prepared yellow mustard (preferably grainy)

½ teaspoon salt

Freshly ground black pepper

1. Bring the water to a boil in a medium saucepan and blanch the asparagus for about 15 seconds. Drain and run it under cold water for 1 minute.

2. To make the sauce, heat the oil in a small saucepan. Add the garlic and cook on low heat for 1 to 2 minutes. Remove from the heat, add the lemon juice, dill, mustard, salt, and pepper to taste, and mix well.

3. Toss the asparagus with the sauce and let stand for 10 minutes before serving.

NOTE: If you bend the stem end of a stalk of asparagus, it will break at precisely the point where it's tender enough to eat. When working with a bunch of asparagus, you don't have to bend every piece individually. Just do one or two, and that will give you an idea of where to cut the rest.

Asparagus with Ginger Sauce

YIELD: 4 SERVINGS

Asparagus especially shines when it is lightly cooked, as in this recipe using traditional Chinese flavors.

1 tablespoon olive oil

1 medium onion, chopped

1 tablespoon peeled and grated fresh ginger

2 to 3 cloves garlic, minced

1 bunch asparagus (about 1 pound), trimmed and chopped

2 tablespoons soy sauce

1 tablespoon rice vinegar

1 teaspoon toasted sesame oil

½ teaspoon unrefined cane sugar

1. Heat the olive oil in a medium saucepan. Add the onion, ginger, and garlic. Cook on medium-low heat for about 5 minutes, or until the onion is translucent.

2. Add the asparagus and soy sauce and cook, stirring occasionally, for 5 to 10 minutes, or until the asparagus are tender.

3. Add the vinegar, sesame oil, and sugar and cook for 2 minutes longer.

Peas and Pea Vines with Fresh Mint

Pea vines have a flavor similar to the peas themselves and complement them nicely. They are traditionally used in Asian stir-fries. Some farmers' market vendors sell them in bunches weighing about a pound, with twisty tendrils that are technically edible, although they are tough to chew. The vines are typically harvested from snow pea plants, although they can come from of any kind of garden pea. You can add tofu to this recipe to turn it into a main dish.

1 tablespoon olive oil

1 medium onion, diced

2 cloves garlic, minced

1 bunch pea vines (about 1 pound; larger stems and tendrils removed), chopped

1 to 2 tablespoons soy sauce

½ cup shelled sugar snap peas

10 to 15 fresh mint leaves, finely chopped

1. Heat the oil in a medium saucepan. Add the onion and garlic. Cook on medium-low heat for about 5 minutes, or until the onion is translucent.

2. Add the pea vines and soy sauce. Cook for about 5 minutes, stirring often.

3. Add the peas and mint and cook for about 5 minutes longer.

Sorrel with Spring Onions

YIELD: 4 SERVINGS

This simple recipe creates a surprising synergy of flavors. Sorrel is a leafy green with a lemony tang. Spring onions are young bulbs, sold with their tender green stems intact.

1 tablespoon olive oil

4 spring onions, including the stems, finely chopped

½ teaspoon salt

2 bunches sorrel (about ½ pound each), chopped

1. Heat the oil in a small saucepan. Add the onions and salt. Cook for about 5 minutes, or until the onions are translucent.

2. Add the sorrel and cook for about 5 minutes longer, or until the greens are very tender. They will turn a brownish color at first, but when they are done, they will look like most other cooked greens.

Pickled Sea Beans

If you live in a coastal area and there's a forager at your local farmers' market, you can get sea beans in the spring and summer. They are gathered from tide pools and are reminiscent of haricots verts, the thinnest, most tender green beans.

½ cup water

¼ cup red wine vinegar

¼ cup olive oil

1 teaspoon salt

1 bunch spring onions, including the stems (about ½ pound), chopped

1 bunch young garlic, including the stems (about ½ pound), chopped

1 pound sea beans, rinsed

1. Bring the water, vinegar, oil, and salt to a boil in a medium saucepan. Add the spring onions and young garlic and cook on medium-low heat for about 5 minutes.

2. Add the sea beans and cook for 5 minutes longer. Serve warm or at room temperature.

Sesame Snow Peas

YIELD: 4 SERVINGS

This simple, flavorful dish works well as a chilled picnic item, or as a warm side dish served with tofu or seitan.

1 pound snow peas, trimmed

2 tablespoons soy sauce

1 tablespoon rice vinegar

1 teaspoon toasted sesame oil

½ teaspoon chili oil

3 green onions, finely chopped

2 tablespoons black sesame seeds

1. Steam the snow peas for 2 minutes.
2. Stir together the soy sauce, rice vinegar, sesame oil, and chili oil in a small bowl.
3. Combine the snow peas, green onions, and black sesame seeds in a medium bowl. Add the soy sauce mixture and toss gently until the vegetables are evenly coated. Taste and add more chili oil, if desired.

Afghani Spinach

In this recipe, spinach is prepared with a blend of spices from a crossroads cuisine linking India and the Middle East.

1 tablespoon olive oil

1 medium onion, chopped

2 cloves garlic, minced

2 bunches spinach (about 1 pound), cleaned and chopped

1 tablespoon chopped fresh cilantro

1 teaspoon dried dill weed

1 teaspoon ground cumin

½ teaspoon ground cardamom

½ teaspoon salt

Juice of ½ lemon

1. Heat the oil in a medium saucepan. Add the onion and garlic. Cook on medium-low heat for about 5 minutes, or until the onion is translucent.

2. Add the spinach, cilantro, dill weed, cumin, cardamom, and salt. Cook for 5 to 10 minutes, stirring often.

3. Stir in the lemon juice and serve.

White Beans with Garlic Scapes

YIELD: 4 SERVINGS

Garlic scapes, also known as garlic stems or tops, are a spring delicacy. They have a texture like green beans, with a mild garlicky flavor.

> 1 to 2 tablespoons olive oil
> 1 bunch garlic scapes (about ½ pound), cut into 1-inch lengths
> ½ teaspoon salt
> 2 cups cooked or canned white beans, drained
> ½ cup finely chopped fresh Italian parsley
> 1 teaspoon freshly squeezed lemon juice

1. Heat the oil in a medium saucepan. Add the garlic scapes and salt. Cook on medium-low heat, stirring often, for about 5 minutes, until the garlic scapes are tender.

2. Add the beans and parsley and cook, stirring occasionally, for about 5 minutes longer, until the beans are heated through.

3. Add the lemon juice and serve.

Tofu Stuffed Lettuce Rolls

These rolls are easy to assemble and require no cooking. You can make them during any season, but I like them best during springtime, when lettuce leaves are most tender.

1 pound soft tofu

2 tablespoons nutritional yeast flakes

1 tablespoon vegan Worcestershire sauce

1 teaspoon dried dill weed

½ teaspoon salt

8 red or green leaf lettuce leaves, washed and dried well

1. To make the filling, mash the tofu. Add the nutritional yeast, Worcestershire sauce, dill weed, and salt and mix well.

2. Trim the tough ends from the lettuce leaves. Lay a leaf in front of you, with the stem facing you. Place one-eighth of the filling in the center of the leaf. Roll up the leaf from the bottom, tucking in the sides toward the center. Continue rolling as tightly as you can. Repeat the process with the remaining lettuce leaves and tofu mixture. Arrange the rolls on a plate with the seams facing down.

Leek and Asparagus Curry

YIELD: 4 SERVINGS

Asparagus season is so fleeting that I like to use the vegetable in every imaginable way. Here it stars in a main dish curry that is filling and satisfying and doesn't take long to prepare. Serve it with basmati rice.

2 tablespoons olive oil

1 tablespoon peeled and grated fresh ginger

4 cloves garlic, minced

1 teaspoon salt

1 teaspoon ground cumin

1 teaspoon ground turmeric

½ teaspoon ground coriander

½ teaspoon ground cardamom

½ teaspoon cayenne (optional)

2 medium leeks, cut in half lengthwise, cleaned well, and sliced

1 bunch asparagus (about 1 pound), trimmed and cut into bite-size pieces

2 cups cooked or canned chickpeas, drained

1 small can (6 ounces) coconut milk

1. Heat the oil in a medium pan. Add the ginger, garlic, salt, cumin, turmeric, coriander, cardamom, and optional cayenne. Cook for 2 to 3 minutes on medium-low heat. Then add the sliced leeks and cook, stirring often, for about 5 minutes, until they are soft.

2. Add the asparagus and cook, stirring often, for about 5 minutes. Then add the chickpeas and cook for 3 to 4 minutes longer, stirring occasionally, until they are heated through.

3. Stir in the coconut milk and cook for about 5 minutes, or until it is hot.

Polenta Primavera

In this recipe, a colorful blend of spring vegetables tops a bed of polenta. The juice from the veggies seeps down into the polenta, making it especially tasty.

3 cups water

2 tablespoons olive oil

1½ teaspoons salt

1 cup yellow corn grits

1 leek, cut in half lengthwise, cleaned well, and chopped

2 cloves garlic, minced

1 bunch red chard (6 to 8 leaves), chopped

1 bunch asparagus (about 1 pound), trimmed and chopped

1 red bell pepper, sliced

½ cup white wine or a nonalcoholic substitute

½ cup chopped fresh parsley

¼ cup chopped fresh chives

1. To make the polenta, combine the water, 1 tablespoon of the oil, and 1 teaspoon of the salt in a small saucepan and bring to a boil. Lower the heat and gradually sprinkle in the corn grits, stirring constantly until the mixture is evenly thick all the way through. Pour into an 8-inch square casserole pan (or anything reasonably close to this size).

2. Heat the remaining tablespoon of oil in a medium saucepan. Add the leek, garlic, and remaining ½ teaspoon of salt. Cook for about 5 minutes, or until the leek is soft and has reduced in size.

3. Add the chard, asparagus, and bell pepper and cook on medium-low heat for about 5 minutes. Add the wine, parsley, and chives and cook 10 minutes longer.

4. Spread the vegetable mixture over the polenta. To serve, cut the polenta into squares or scoop it out with a serving spoon.

Baby Bok Choy with Tofu

YIELD: 4 SERVINGS

Baby bok choy is a versatile vegetable. At farmers' markets it's usually sold in bunches of about a pound, made up of several small heads. This simple recipe offers it seasoned with traditional Chinese flavors. Serve it with noodles or rice.

1 to 2 tablespoons olive oil

1 leek, cut in half lengthwise, cleaned well, and sliced

2 tablespoons peeled and grated fresh ginger

4 cloves garlic, minced

1 bunch baby bok choy (about 1 pound), trimmed and chopped

½ pound firm tofu, cut into 1-inch cubes

2 to 3 tablespoons soy sauce

1 teaspoon toasted sesame oil

1. Heat the olive oil in a large skillet. Add the leek, ginger, and garlic. Cook for about 5 minutes on medium-low heat, until the leek is soft.

2. Add the baby bok choy and cook for about 5 minutes, until the white parts of the stems are just tender.

3. Add the tofu and soy sauce and cook for about 5 minutes longer, or until the tofu is heated through. Add the sesame oil and serve.

Pea and Radish Salad

Fresh peas have so much sweetness and vitality. In this recipe they are paired with crunchy spring radishes, cut to the same size as the peas.

1 cup shelled English peas

8 to 10 radishes, trimmed and diced about the same size as the peas

2 tablespoons chopped fresh chives

1 tablespoon olive oil

1 tablespoon balsamic vinegar

½ teaspoon salt

Freshly ground black pepper

Combine all of the ingredients and mix well.

Solstice
Steamed Vegetable Salad

YIELD: 6 SERVINGS

A group of friends and I have a potluck picnic every year on the summer solstice and watch the late sunset over the water and mountains. This was my contribution one year, conceived specially for the occasion.

> 1 bunch red chard (4 to 6 leaves), trimmed and chopped
>
> 2 cups broccoli florets
>
> 2 carrots, peeled (if desired) and sliced
>
> 1 cup snow peas, trimmed
>
> ½ cup peas (preferably freshly shelled)
>
> 1 quart water
>
> 1 cup uncooked orzo
>
> ¼ cup chopped fresh basil
>
> 2 tablespoons chopped fresh chives
>
> 2 tablespoons red wine vinegar
>
> 2 tablespoons olive oil
>
> 1 teaspoon salt
>
> Freshly ground black pepper

1. Using a vegetable steamer, separately steam each kind of vegetable for a few minutes, until tender but still colorful. Gently toss the steamed vegetables together in a large bowl.

2. While the vegetables are steaming, boil the water for the orzo in a medium saucepan. Add the orzo and cook for about 5 minutes, stirring almost constantly. Drain and rinse with cold water.

3. Add the orzo to the steamed vegetables along with all of the remaining ingredients and toss gently until well combined.

YIELD: 4 SERVINGS

Persian Radishes and Nuts

I learned a version of this salad from a Persian friend. In the authentic recipe, the different ingredients (except for the salt, lemon juice, and olive oil, which are my own additions) are laid side by side so guests can take some of whatever they like and roll it in lavash, a traditional flatbread. I mix everything together, because it's easier to serve.

8 to 10 radishes, trimmed and sliced

1 bunch green onions, finely chopped (about 1 cup)

½ cup chopped walnuts or almonds

¼ cup chopped fresh parsley

2 tablespoons chopped fresh mint

2 tablespoons olive oil

Juice of ½ lemon

½ teaspoon salt

Combine all of the ingredients and mix well.

Strawberry-Rhubarb Tart

YIELD: 8 SERVINGS

This recipe uses the classic combination of strawberries and rhubarb on top of a shortbread crust. It's best if you serve it warm, right out of the oven.

CRUST

1 cup nonhydrogenated margarine

1 cup unrefined cane sugar

2 cups unbleached white or whole wheat flour

½ teaspoon baking soda

TOPPING

½ cup fruit juice (any kind except citrus)

1 pint strawberries, hulled and sliced

1 stalk rhubarb, finely chopped

2 to 3 tablespoons sweetener of your choice

1 teaspoon vanilla extract

2 to 3 tablespoons white or brown rice flour

1. Preheat the oven to 375 degrees F.

2. To make the crust, combine the margarine and sugar in a medium bowl. Then stir in the wheat flour and baking soda until well combined. Spread this mixture on the bottom of an 8-inch square baking pan and bake it for 20 to 30 minutes, until it's just firm to the touch.

3. To make the topping, gently heat the juice in a medium saucepan. Add the strawberries, rhubarb, sweetener, and vanilla extract. Cook on medium-low heat for a few minutes, until the berries start to break down. Sprinkle in the rice flour a little at a time, stirring constantly until the mixture thickens.

4. Spoon the fruit mixture on top of the crust and bake for about 5 minutes.

Chocolate-Dipped Strawberries

If you use fine chocolate for this recipe, it will be exquisite. If you use ordinary chocolate, it will still be quite good.

1 bar (2½ ounces) dark chocolate

1 pint strawberries

1. Melt the chocolate in a double boiler. If you don't have a double boiler, you can improvise by fitting a metal bowl over a saucepan holding 1 inch of gently boiling water.

2. Dip each strawberry into the melted chocolate, coating the berry but not the hull. Lay the coated berries on a sheet of waxed paper to cool. They'll be ready to serve once the chocolate has set. You can put them in the refrigerator if you are in a hurry.

Summer

Summer produce is abundant and flamboyant, ripe and ready and easy to use. It's a time for raw salads, to take the edge off the heat. Summer recipes show off the wonderful flavors and textures of the season, which often need little adornment. Think of a perfectly ripe peach, with its juice running down your chin, or a plump tomato with just a sprinkle of salt. It's the season for picnic food, barbecues, and eating outdoors. It's also the easiest time to eat locally, with farmers' markets and Community Supported Agriculture (CSA) programs in full swing, and plenty of great weather to enjoy them.

Summer Produce

EARLY SUMMER	MIDSUMMER	LATE SUMMER
fennel	apricots	corn
green beans	arugula	eggplants
lettuce	basil	melons
new potatoes	blackberries	nectarines
raspberries	blueberries	peaches
	cucumbers	
	fava beans	
	okra	
	onions	
	peppers	
	purslane	
	squash blossoms	
	summer squash	
	tomatoes	
	zucchini	

Quick Tomato Sauce

YIELD: ABOUT 2 CUPS

This recipe is a perfect example of how you don't need to fuss with your food if your ingredients are just right. Midsummer tomatoes and basil: what more could you possibly need?

2 tablespoons olive oil

4 cloves garlic, minced

4 ripe tomatoes, diced

½ teaspoon salt

Freshly ground black pepper

½ cup chopped fresh basil

1. Heat the oil in a medium saucepan on medium-low heat. Add the garlic and cook for about 1 minute.

2. Add the tomatoes, salt, and pepper to taste. Cook on medium heat, stirring often, for 5 to 10 minutes, or until the tomatoes start to break down.

3. Add the basil and cook for 2 to 3 minutes longer.

Puttanesca Sauce

Here is a tasty variation of a simple tomato sauce.

2 tablespoons olive oil

4 cloves garlic, minced

¼ cup sliced olives (green or black, or a combination)

2 tablespoons capers

4 ripe tomatoes, diced

¼ cup chopped fresh parsley

½ teaspoon salt

Freshly ground black pepper

1. Heat the oil in a small saucepan on medium-low heat. Add the garlic and cook for 1 minute.

2. Add the olives and capers and cook for 1 to 2 minutes, until they are heated through.

3. Add the tomatoes, parsley, salt, and pepper to taste and cook on medium heat for about 5 minutes, until the tomatoes break down.

Caponata

This is an eggplant-tomato relish that you can use as a sauce for pasta or polenta, or as a topping for bruschetta.

2 to 3 tablespoons olive oil

1 eggplant, cut into 1-inch cubes

1 medium onion, chopped

2 cloves garlic, minced

2 ripe tomatoes, chopped

2 tablespoons chopped fresh basil

½ teaspoon salt

12 to 15 pitted kalamata olives, sliced

2 tablespoons pine nuts

1 tablespoon red wine vinegar

1. Heat the olive oil in a medium saucepan. Add the eggplant, onion, and garlic and cook on medium-low heat, stirring often, for 10 to 15 minutes, or until the eggplant is soft.

2. Add the tomatoes, basil, and salt and cook, stirring occasionally, about 10 minutes longer, or until the tomatoes break down.

3. Remove from the heat and stir in the olives, pine nuts, and vinegar.

Sicilian Pesto

The Sicilian version of basil pesto uses a bit of fresh tomato along with the basil, nuts, and garlic.

3 cloves garlic, peeled
2 cups fresh basil leaves
1 ripe tomato, coarsely chopped
¼ cup walnuts or pine nuts
2 to 3 tablespoons olive oil
½ teaspoon salt
Freshly ground black pepper

1. Chop the garlic in a food processor.
2. Add all of the remaining ingredients and process until smooth.

Fennel and Arugula Pesto

YIELD: ABOUT 1 CUP

This spicy, verdant sauce makes a great topping for pasta, or you can toast slices of bread and use it to make bruschetta.

6 cloves garlic, unpeeled

¼ cup olive oil

½ cup walnuts

½ cup coarsely chopped fennel bulb

2 cups arugula

1 tablespoon balsamic vinegar

½ teaspoon salt

1. Preheat the oven to 400 degrees F.

2. Rub the garlic cloves with enough of the oil to coat them. Wrap them in foil and roast them in the oven for 25 to 35 minutes, or until they are soft enough that you can squeeze the pulp out of the skins.

3. When the garlic cloves are cool enough to handle, squeeze out the pulp into a food processor. Add the remaining oil and all of the walnuts and fennel. Process until the walnuts and fennel are coarsely chopped.

4. Add half of the arugula and process until it is fairly smooth. Then add the remaining arugula along with all of the balsamic vinegar and salt and process until smooth.

Green Bean–Walnut Pâté

YIELD: ABOUT 1 CUP

You can spread this pâté on bread or crackers, or use it to stuff almost anything that can be stuffed.

6 cloves garlic, unpeeled

2 tablespoons olive oil

½ pound green beans

½ cup walnuts

½ cup chopped fresh parsley

Juice of ½ lemon, or 2 tablespoons balsamic or red wine vinegar

½ teaspoon salt

1. Preheat the oven to 400 degrees F.

2. Rub the garlic cloves with enough of the oil to coat them. Wrap them in foil and roast them in the oven for 25 to 35 minutes, or until they are soft enough that you can squeeze the pulp out of the skins.

3. While the garlic is roasting, trim the green beans, cut them in half, and steam them for about 3 minutes.

4. When the garlic cloves are cool enough to handle, squeeze out the pulp into a food processor. Add the green beans and all of the remaining ingredients and process until the mixture is fairly smooth.

Peach Salsa

This is a classic salsa recipe with the sweet bonus of a ripe summer peach.

1 pasilla, poblano, or Anaheim chile
1 jalapeño chile
1 teaspoon olive oil
3 ripe tomatoes
1 ripe peach
¼ cup chopped fresh cilantro
2 tablespoons red wine vinegar
½ teaspoon salt

1. Preheat the oven to 400 degrees F.

2. Using your hands, rub the chiles with the oil. Arrange them on a baking sheet along with the whole tomatoes and the peach. Roast them for about 1 hour, or until the chiles droop and their skins turn brown.

3. When they are cool enough to handle, remove the stems from the chiles, the cores from the tomatoes, and the pit from the peach.

4. Place the chiles, tomatoes, and peach in a food processor or blender. Add the cilantro, vinegar, and salt and process until smooth.

Green Bean and New Potato Soup

YIELD: 4 SERVINGS

Here is a soup for the occasional cool summer day. It uses the tender potatoes that appear early in the season.

4 cups unsalted vegetable stock or water

½ pound new potatoes, quartered

1 medium onion, chopped

½ cup white wine or a nonalcoholic substitute

½ cup chopped fresh parsley

¼ cup nutritional yeast flakes

6 cloves garlic, minced

1 teaspoon salt

½ teaspoon freshly ground black pepper

2 cups chopped green beans

½ cup chopped fresh dill

Juice of 1 lemon

1. Bring the stock to a boil in a medium soup pot. Add the potatoes, onion, wine, parsley, nutritional yeast, garlic, salt, and pepper. Bring back to a boil, lower the heat, and cook for about 30 minutes, or until the potatoes are tender.

2. Add the green beans, dill, and lemon juice and cook for about 5 minutes longer.

Minestrone

This is a traditional Italian soup. Serve it with any pasta or polenta dish.

1 tablespoon olive oil

1 medium onion, chopped

3 cloves garlic, minced

1 cup chopped green beans

2 tablespoons chopped fresh basil

1 teaspoon dried oregano

1 teaspoon salt

6 large ripe tomatoes, coarsely chopped

1 cup cooked or canned kidney beans or chickpeas, drained

1 cup cooked small pasta (preferably elbow macaroni or small shells)

1. Heat the oil in a medium saucepan or small soup pot. Add the onion, and garlic and cook on medium-low heat for about 5 minutes. Add the green beans, basil, oregano, and salt and cook for 5 minutes.

2. Add the tomatoes and cook on medium-low heat for about 15 minutes, until they start to break down.

3. Add the beans and pasta and cook for about 5 minutes longer.

Squash Blossoms with Chiles

YIELD: 4 SERVINGS

Squash blossoms have a delicate texture, and their bright orange hue makes a colorful dish. They are often sold by the pound at farmers' markets from midsummer to early fall. They'll keep for a couple of days in the refrigerator. You can serve this dish on its own or as a filling for tacos, burritos, tamales, or enchiladas.

1 tablespoon olive oil

3 to 4 cloves garlic, minced

2 medium zucchini or pattypan squash, finely chopped

1 pasilla, poblano, or Anaheim chile, finely chopped

1 teaspoon chili powder (mild or hot)

½ teaspoon ground cumin

½ teaspoon dried oregano

½ teaspoon salt

½ pound squash blossoms, rinsed

2 tablespoons chopped fresh cilantro

Juice of ¼ lime

1. Heat the oil in a medium saucepan. Add the garlic and cook for about 1 minute.

2. Add the zucchini, chile, chili powder, cumin, oregano, and salt. Cook on medium-low heat for 3 to 4 minutes, until the vegetables are just tender.

3. Add the squash blossoms and cilantro and cook for 1 to 2 minutes longer, taking care not to overcook the squash blossoms.

4. Stir in the lime juice and serve.

Okra with Tomatoes

YIELD: 4 SERVINGS

Okra is a deeply misunderstood vegetable, probably because it is prone to sliminess when it is overcooked. It has a delightful texture and flavor if you don't overdo it.

1 tablespoon olive oil

3 cloves garlic, minced

1 pound okra, trimmed and cut into bite-size pieces

½ teaspoon salt

2 ripe tomatoes, diced

¼ cup chopped fresh parsley

1. Heat the oil in a medium saucepan. Add the garlic and cook for about 1 minute.

2. Add the okra and salt and cook on medium-low heat for 3 to 4 minutes.

3. Add the tomatoes and parsley and cook for about 5 minutes longer, until the tomatoes start to break down.

Haricots Verts with Slivered Almonds

YIELD: 4 SERVINGS

Haricots verts are an especially small and tender variety of green bean. In this recipe, the thin slices of red pepper colorfully mirror their shape.

2 cups trimmed haricots verts

1 red bell pepper, cut into small slivers

½ cup slivered almonds

¼ cup chopped fresh parsley

2 tablespoons olive oil

2 teaspoons freshly squeezed lemon juice

½ teaspoon salt

1. Steam the haricots verts and bell pepper for about 1 minute. They should be just tender and still colorful. Rinse them under cold water and drain well.

2. Transfer the steamed vegetables to a bowl. Add the almonds, parsley, oil, lemon juice, and salt and toss until evenly combined.

Morel Mushrooms with New Potatoes and Fresh Peas

YIELD: 4 SERVINGS

Choose the smallest potatoes you can find for this recipe. This dish has a depth of flavor that you usually find in fall and winter foods, but it uses ingredients unique to early summertime.

1 to 2 tablespoons olive oil

12 medium morel mushrooms, finely chopped

1 small onion, diced

4 cloves garlic, minced

½ teaspoon salt

Freshly ground black pepper

½ pound new potatoes, cut in half

¼ cup Marsala wine or unsalted vegetable stock

½ cup shelled English peas

1. Heat the oil in a medium saucepan. Add the mushrooms, onion, garlic, salt, and pepper to taste. Cook on medium-low heat for about 5 minutes, or until the onion is translucent.

2. Add the potatoes and wine, lower the heat, cover, and cook for about 10 minutes. Uncover and cook for 5 minutes longer, stirring often, until the potatoes are tender.

3. Remove from the heat, add the peas, cover, and let stand for a few minutes before serving. The peas should be heated through but not cooked.

Pesto Stuffed Tomatoes

YIELD: 4 SERVINGS

These stuffed tomatoes make a great appetizer. They offer a delightful blend of textures, with a crunchy breading on top of the juicy ripe tomatoes.

    2 tablespoons olive oil

    2 tablespoons Sicilian Pesto (page 55)

    ½ cup bread crumbs

    2 ripe tomatoes

1. Preheat the oven to 375 degrees F.

2. Heat the oil in a small saucepan. Add the Sicilian Pesto. Cook on low heat for 2 to 3 minutes, stirring almost constantly. Stir in the bread crumbs and remove from the heat.

3. Cut the tomatoes in half horizontally. Cover the smooth surface of each half with the bread crumb mixture, rounding it with a spoon.

4. Arrange the tomatoes on a baking sheet and bake in the oven for 30 to 40 minutes, or until the bread crumb topping starts to brown.

Fried Green Tomatoes

Here is a vegan version of this traditional Southern staple. Try these tart, crispy treats with Peach Salsa (page 58).

2 tablespoons olive oil

2 tablespoons unbleached white or whole wheat flour

2 tablespoons nutritional yeast flakes

¾ cup water

1 teaspoon prepared yellow mustard

½ teaspoon salt

2 large green (unripe) tomatoes

2 cups masa harina

¼ cup canola oil (or any high-quality oil except olive oil)

1. Heat the olive oil gently in a small saucepan. Add the flour and nutritional yeast and mix until smooth. Gradually beat in the water, taking care to avoid lumps. Bring to a boil, stirring almost constantly. Cook and stir on low heat for about 30 seconds, or until the mixture thickens. Remove from the heat and stir in the mustard and salt.

2. Cut the tomatoes in slices ¼ to ½ inch thick. Pour the flour mixture into a bowl and spread the masa harina on a plate. Dip each tomato slice first in the flour mixture and then in the masa harina, turning it over to coat both sides.

3. Heat the canola oil gently in a medium skillet. It should be hot enough to sizzle when you drop in a cube of bread, but not hot enough to smoke. Gently place the breaded tomato slices in the oil, a few at a time. Use a pair of tongs to turn them after 1 to 2 minutes. Cook them until the breading is golden brown on both sides.

Zucchini Piccata

These crispy breaded zucchini sticks make a fun side dish. You can serve them with marinara sauce on the side for dipping, or arrange them artfully on top of any pasta dish.

> 3 tablespoons water
>
> 3 tablespoons olive oil
>
> 2 tablespoons tahini
>
> 1 teaspoon freshly squeezed lemon juice
>
> 1 teaspoon dried parsley flakes
>
> ½ teaspoon salt
>
> ¼ cup cracker crumbs
>
> ¼ cup raw sunflower seeds, coarsely ground in a food processor
>
> ¼ teaspoon baking powder
>
> 2 medium zucchini, cut into finger-size sticks

1. Preheat the oven to 400 degrees F and oil a baking sheet.

2. Combine the water, 1 tablespoon of the oil, all of the tahini, lemon juice, and parsley flakes, and a pinch of the salt in a small bowl.

3. In a separate small bowl, combine the cracker crumbs, sunflower seeds, baking powder, and the remaining salt.

4. Dip each zucchini stick first in the tahini mixture and then in the cracker crumb mixture. Arrange the breaded sticks on the prepared baking sheet and brush them gently with the remaining oil. Bake for about 20 minutes, or until they start to brown.

Panfried Baby Artichokes with Basil "Mayonnaise"

YIELD: 4 SERVINGS

Baby artichokes—those that are about the size of a golf ball—don't have a choke, the gristly center that you have to scrape off of a bigger artichoke to get to the heart. The small ones cook in just a few minutes in a little bit of oil. They make a great appetizer or side dish.

6 baby artichokes

3 tablespoons olive oil

¾ teaspoon salt

¼ teaspoon freshly ground black pepper

¼ pound soft tofu

6 to 8 fresh basil leaves

1 teaspoon freshly squeezed lemon juice

1. Cut the artichokes in half lengthwise. Trim the pointy edges off the tops and about ¼ inch off the bottoms.

2. Heat 2 tablespoons of the oil in a medium skillet. Then arrange as many artichoke halves as you can comfortably fit in the pan, with their flat sides facing down. Cook them for about 5 minutes, until the surfaces touching the pan start to brown. Turn them over, sprinkle them with salt and pepper (use ½ teaspoon of the salt for all of the artichokes), and cook for 2 to 3 minutes on the other side. Repeat with the remaining artichokes.

3. To make the basil "mayonnaise," combine the remaining tablespoon of olive oil with the tofu, basil, lemon juice, and the remaining ¼ teaspoon of salt in a food processor and process until smooth. Arrange the artichokes on a plate with the basil "mayonnaise" in a small bowl in the center.

Fried Okra

YIELD: 4 SERVINGS

Here is another Southern favorite: breaded fresh okra, crispy on the outside, with the insides cooked until just tender.

2 tablespoons olive oil

2 tablespoons unbleached white or whole wheat flour

2 tablespoons nutritional yeast flakes

¾ cup water

½ teaspoon salt

1 teaspoon prepared yellow mustard

1 pound okra

2 cups masa harina

¼ cup canola oil (or any high-quality oil except olive oil)

1. Heat the olive oil gently in a small saucepan. Add the flour and nutritional yeast and mix until smooth. Gradually stir in the water, taking care to avoid any lumps. Bring to a boil, stirring almost constantly. Cook and stir on low heat for about 30 seconds, or until the mixture thickens. Remove from the heat and stir in the salt and mustard.

2. Pour the flour mixture into a bowl and spread the masa harina on a plate. Dip each piece of okra first in the flour mixture and then in the masa harina, rolling it to coat it all over.

3. Heat the canola oil gently in a medium skillet. It should be hot enough to sizzle when you drop in a cube of bread, but not hot enough to smoke. Gently place the breaded okra in the oil, a few pieces at a time. Use a pair of tongs to turn them over after 1 to 2 minutes. Cook until the breading is golden brown all over.

Herb-Roasted Corn on the Cob

YIELD: 6 SERVINGS

Here is a new twist on a classic summer favorite. You can roast the corn in the oven or cook it outdoors on the grill.

6 cloves garlic, unpeeled

2 tablespoons olive oil

½ cup chopped fresh parsley

½ teaspoon salt

3 ears corn, shucked and cut in half widthwise

1. Preheat the oven to 400 degrees F.

2. Rub the garlic cloves with enough of the oil to coat them. Wrap them in foil and roast them in the oven for 25 to 35 minutes, or until they are soft enough that you can squeeze the pulp out of the skins.

3. When the garlic cloves are cool enough to handle, squeeze out the pulp into a food processor or blender. Add the remaining olive oil and all of the parsley and salt and process until smooth.

4. Generously coat the corn with the garlic mixture (a pastry brush works well). Arrange the pieces on a baking sheet and roast in the oven for about 30 minutes.

Stuffed Baby Pattypans

YIELD: 15 SMALL SERVINGS

These stuffed baby squash are a fun finger food. Use as many different colors as you can find.

> 6½ cups water
>
> ¼ cup quinoa
>
> 15 baby pattypan squash (about 1 ounce each)
>
> 1 tablespoon olive oil
>
> 2 cloves garlic, minced
>
> 2 to 3 tablespoons chopped hazelnuts
>
> 2 to 3 tablespoons chopped fresh parsley
>
> ½ teaspoon salt
>
> 6 to 8 dried tomatoes, boiled for 1 minute, drained, and finely chopped

1. Bring ½ cup of the water to a boil in a small saucepan. Stir in the quinoa, lower the heat, cover, and cook for about 15 minutes, until all of the water is absorbed.

2. Trim just enough from the bottoms of the squash to make them sit flat. Cut the stems from the tops. Scoop a small teaspoon of pulp from the top center of each one. Finely chop the pulp and set it aside.

3. Bring the remaining 6 cups of water to a boil in a medium saucepan. Immerse the squash in the boiling water for about 1 minute, or long enough to just soften them. Drain them and run cold water over them.

4. Preheat the oven to 375 degrees F.

5. Heat the oil in a small saucepan. Add the garlic and cook on medium-low heat for 1 to 2 minutes. Add the chopped squash pulp, hazelnuts, parsley, and salt and cook for 2 minutes. Remove from the heat, add the dried tomatoes and quinoa, and mix well.

6. Stuff about 1 teaspoon of the quinoa mixture into the top of each squash, rounding it with a spoon. Arrange the stuffed squash on a baking sheet.

7. Bake for 10 to 15 minutes, or just long enough for the squash to be heated through.

Kappa Maki (CUCUMBER SUSHI ROLL)

YIELD: 6 ROLLS

(50 to 60 bite-size pieces)

These rolls are prettiest if you use pristine white rice; but if you are passionate about whole grains, you can substitute brown rice. I recommend using a sushi mat, but you can manage just fine even if you don't have one, especially once you get a bit of practice. Serve these rolls with extra soy sauce, pickled ginger, and wasabi horseradish.

2 cups water

1 cup white or brown short-grain rice

¼ cup rice vinegar

1 teaspoon unrefined cane sugar

1 cucumber

6 sheets toasted nori

2 teaspoons soy sauce

1. Bring the water to a boil in a small saucepan. Stir in the rice, lower the heat, cover, and cook until all of the water is absorbed, about 20 to 30 minutes for white rice, or 30 to 40 minutes for brown rice.

2. Stir the vinegar and sugar into the rice, and spread it 1 inch thick on a plate to cool quickly.

3. Peel the cucumber and cut it into wedges about the size of a finger.

4. Lay a sheet of nori horizontally over a sushi mat. Spread about ½ cup of the rice in a horizontal layer 2 to 3 inches wide, starting about 1 inch from the bottom. Lay 2 to 3 cucumber wedges end to end on top of the rice, so that they reach from one end of the sheet to the other. Roll the bottom of the mat toward the center to shape the roll, then unroll the mat and roll the nori the rest of the way. If you are not using a mat, you can just roll the bottom up, shape it with your hands to make sure it's as tight as possible, then continue rolling. Spread a thin layer of soy sauce horizontally near the top end of the nori to help seal the rolls.

5. Repeat the process with the remaining rice mixture, cucumber, nori, and soy sauce. Slice each roll into 8 or 10 pieces.

Summer Squash with Basil

YIELD: 4 SERVINGS

To make this dish most appealing, use a colorful variety of summer squash, from yellow crooknecks to zucchini to pattypans.

    1 tablespoon olive oil
    2 cloves garlic, minced
    1 pound summer squash, cut into bite-size pieces
    1 ripe tomato, cut into bite-size pieces
    ¼ cup chopped fresh basil
    ½ teaspoon salt

1. Heat the oil in a medium saucepan on medium-low heat. Add the garlic and cook for about 1 minute.
2. Add the remaining ingredients and cook, stirring often, for about 10 minutes, or until the squash is soft.

Balsamic Cipollini Onions

YIELD: ABOUT 20 SERVINGS

(20 bite-size pieces)

Cipollini onions are bite-size cocktail onions. In this recipe, they are lightly cooked in a glaze made from balsamic vinegar. They make a tasty addition to salads or a great picnic side dish. They will keep for about two weeks in the refrigerator.

1 cup water	1 teaspoon salt
½ cup balsamic vinegar	½ pound cipollini onions, peeled

1. Combine the water, vinegar, and salt in a small saucepan and bring to a boil. Add the onions and bring the mixture back to a boil.
2. Lower the heat and simmer for about 30 minutes. Store the onions in the reduced vinegar mixture in the refrigerator. Serve chilled.

Greek Stewed Vegetables

This recipe shows off mixed vegetables in a sauce of tomato and dill. Serve it with Stuffed Eggplant (page 78).

1 tablespoon olive oil

2 cloves garlic, minced

2 carrots, peeled (if desired) and chopped

2 medium zucchini, sliced

1 cup chopped green beans

3 ripe tomatoes, coarsely chopped

1 teaspoon dried dill weed

1 teaspoon salt

Juice of ½ lemon

1. Heat the oil in a medium saucepan on low heat. Add the garlic and cook for about 1 minute.

2. Add the carrots and cook for about 5 minutes, stirring often. Then add the zucchini and green beans and cook for another 5 minutes, stirring often.

3. Add the tomatoes, dill weed, and salt and cook on medium-low heat for 10 to 15 minutes longer, stirring occasionally, until the tomatoes break down and the vegetables are tender.

4. Stir in the lemon juice and serve.

Dilly Beans

I love the taste of pickled foods, but I'm not meticulous enough to try my hand at canning. My compromise is to cook foods as if I'd be pickling them and store them in the refrigerator. They keep for about two weeks, but I always finish mine long before that. Eat these green beans chilled, as a picnic item.

2 cups water

⅔ cup white vinegar

2 to 3 tablespoons olive oil

6 cloves garlic, peeled

Several sprigs fresh dill, or 2 teaspoons dried dill weed

1 teaspoon salt

1 pound green beans, trimmed

1. Combine the water, vinegar, oil, whole garlic cloves, dill, and salt in a medium saucepan and bring to a boil.

2. Add the green beans, bring the mixture back to a boil, lower the heat, and simmer for about 5 minutes. Store the green beans in their cooking liquid in the refrigerator. Serve chilled.

Summer Vegetable Medley

Vegetables are at their best this time of year and need little to complement them. You can use bell peppers or sweet Gypsy peppers. Add anything else that looks appealing as well.

2 tablespoons olive oil

1 medium onion (ideally a fresh one, with its stem attached), finely chopped

1 medium or 2 small sweet peppers, diced

½ cup chopped fennel bulb

4 cloves garlic, minced

½ teaspoon salt

¼ pound green beans, trimmed and cut in half

1 cup fresh corn kernels (2 to 3 ears)

1 pint cherry tomatoes, cut in half

1 tablespoon balsamic vinegar (optional)

1. Heat the oil in a medium skillet. Add the onion, pepper(s), fennel, garlic, and salt. Cook, stirring occasionally, for about 10 minutes, or until the fennel is soft and the onion is translucent.

2. Add the green beans, corn, and cherry tomatoes and cook, stirring often, for about 10 minutes longer. Remove from the heat and stir in the balsamic vinegar, if desired.

Green Beans with Chickpeas

YIELD: 4 SERVINGS

This satisfying main dish features stewed green beans with chickpeas and traditional Italian flavors. Serve it with rice, pasta, or polenta.

1 tablespoon olive oil

4 cloves garlic, minced

2 cups chopped green beans

1 ripe tomato, chopped

½ cup chopped fresh Italian parsley

½ teaspoon salt

Freshly ground black pepper

2 cups canned or cooked chickpeas, drained

1. Heat the oil in a medium saucepan. Add the garlic and cook for 1 minute on medium-low heat. Add the green beans and cook for about 5 minutes, stirring often. Add the tomato, parsley, salt, and pepper to taste and cook, stirring often, for 5 to 10 minutes, or until the tomato breaks down.

2. Add the chickpeas and cook for about 5 minutes longer, until they are heated through.

Stuffed Eggplant

YIELD: 6 SERVINGS

These eggplants are stuffed with rice and lentils, seasoned with light Middle Eastern flavors. You can serve them as an entrée, or cut them into smaller pieces and present them as an appetizer.

1½ cups water

¾ cup short-grain brown rice

3 medium eggplants

3 to 4 tablespoons olive oil

1 medium onion, chopped

2 cloves garlic, minced

2 cups cooked or canned lentils, drained

¼ cup chopped fresh parsley

2 tablespoons freshly squeezed lemon juice

1 tablespoon chopped fresh spearmint, or 1 teaspoon dried

1. Bring the water to a boil in a small saucepan. Stir in the rice, return to a boil, lower the heat, cover, and cook for 30 to 40 minutes, until all of the water is absorbed.

2. Meanwhile, preheat the oven to 375 degrees F.

3. Slice the eggplants in half lengthwise and brush each half with some of the oil. Place on a baking sheet and bake for 40 to 60 minutes, or until they are soft.

4. While the eggplant and rice are cooking, heat the remainder of the oil in a small saucepan. Add the onion and garlic and cook for 5 minutes, or until the onion is translucent. When the rice is ready, stir in the onion and garlic. Then add the lentils, parsley, lemon juice, and spearmint.

5. When the eggplants are cool enough to handle, scoop out as much of the pulp as you can without tearing the skins. Chop the pulp, add it to the lentil mixture, and stuff it gently into the eggplant skins.

6. Arrange the stuffed eggplants on the baking sheet and bake for 10 to 15 minutes.

Yemenite Lentil Stew

YIELD: 6 SERVINGS

The seasonings in this stew come from an ancient North African cuisine.

2½ cups water

1 cup dried lentils

¼ cup chopped fresh parsley

¼ cup chopped fresh cilantro

1 jalapeño chile, minced

1 tablespoon ground cumin

1 teaspoon salt

1 tablespoon olive oil

1 medium onion, chopped

2 cloves garlic, minced

1 medium eggplant, cut into 1-inch cubes

2 carrots, peeled (if desired) and chopped

1 zucchini, chopped

1. Bring the water to a boil in a medium soup pot and add the lentils, parsley, cilantro, chile, cumin, and ½ teaspoon of the salt.

2. While the lentils are cooking, heat the olive oil in a medium saucepan. Add the onion and garlic and the remaining ½ teaspoon of salt. Cook on medium-low heat for about 5 minutes, or until the onion is translucent. Add the eggplant and cook for about 10 minutes, stirring often. Then add the carrots and zucchini and cook for about 10 minutes longer, or until all of the vegetables are tender.

3. When the lentils are soft, add the vegetables and cook on low heat for 5 minutes.

Summer Stuffed Cabbage

We tend to associate stuffed cabbage with cold climates and wintry days, but cabbage is also abundant during the early summer. In this recipe, it is stuffed with a light rice pilaf and a sauce made from fresh tomatoes.

1½ cups water

¾ cup short-grain brown rice

1 tablespoon olive oil

1 small onion, finely chopped

4 cloves garlic, minced

¼ cup chopped fresh parsley

1 tablespoon finely chopped fresh spearmint, or 1 teaspoon dried

½ teaspoon salt

3 ripe tomatoes, diced

2 tablespoons raw sunflower seeds

1 medium head cabbage

1. Bring the water to a boil in a small saucepan. Stir in the rice, return to a boil, lower the heat, cover, and cook for 30 to 40 minutes, until all of the water is absorbed.

2. Meanwhile, heat the oil in a small saucepan and add the onion, garlic, parsley, mint, and salt. Cook on medium-low heat, stirring occasionally, for about 5 minutes, or until the onion is translucent. Add the tomatoes and cook, stirring often, for about 5 minutes, until they start to break down.

3. When the rice is ready, mix it with the sunflower seeds and half of the tomato mixture. Set the rest of the tomato mixture aside.

4. Preheat the oven to 375 degrees F.

5. Bring 2 to 3 quarts of water to a boil in a large stockpot. Immerse the head of cabbage, holding it under the water with a pair of tongs. After about 2 minutes, remove and drain it. When it is cool enough to handle, gently peel off the outer leaves. If you don't get 8 intact leaves about the size of your hand, submerge the head again and peel off a few more leaves as they soften.

6. Trim the stiff part from the bottom of each leaf. Place a few tablespoons of the rice mixture in the center of 1 leaf. Roll it up from the bottom, folding the sides over and in as you continue rolling. Repeat with the remaining leaves and the remaining filling.

7. Place the rolls in an 8-inch square baking dish with the seams facing down and cover them with the remaining tomato mixture. Cover the dish with foil and bake for about 30 minutes, or until the cabbage is very soft.

Armenian Stewed Eggplant

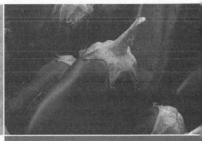

YIELD: 4 SERVINGS

In this recipe, eggplant is stewed in a tomato sauce delicately seasoned with orange juice, basil, and mint.

1 tablespoon olive oil, or more as needed

1 medium onion, chopped

2 cloves garlic, minced

1 teaspoon salt

1 medium eggplant, cut into bite-size cubes

1 tablespoon dried basil

1 tablespoon chopped fresh spearmint, or 1 teaspoon dried

4 ripe tomatoes, chopped

¼ cup orange juice

1. Heat the oil in a medium saucepan. Add the onion, garlic, and salt and cook for about 5 minutes, or until the onion is translucent.

2. Add the eggplant, basil, and mint, and cook on medium heat, stirring often, for 10 to 20 minutes, until the eggplant is soft. Add more oil as needed.

3. When the eggplant is soft, add the tomatoes and cook on medium-low heat, stirring occasionally, for 10 to 15 minutes, until they start to break down. Stir in the orange juice and serve.

Pasta with Wilted Arugula and Cherry Tomatoes

YIELD: 4 SERVINGS

Arugula is a spicy green that's usually eaten in cold salads. In this recipe it is mixed with warm ingredients, but it is not quite cooked, preserving the flavor while softening it a bit.

> 2 tablespoons olive oil
>
> 4 cloves garlic, minced
>
> 2 cups cherry tomatoes, cut in half
>
> 1 teaspoon salt
>
> 2 cups arugula
>
> 2 quarts water
>
> 1 pound broad pasta (such as tagliatelle or pappardelle)

1. Heat the oil in a medium saucepan. Add the garlic and cook on medium-low heat for 1 minute. Add the cherry tomatoes and salt and cook for 2 to 3 minutes. Remove from the heat and add the arugula.

2. Bring the water to a boil in a medium saucepan and cook the pasta for 6 to 8 minutes, or until it is tender. Drain the pasta well and combine it with the arugula mixture.

Lentils with Fennel and Sweet Peppers

YIELD: 4 SERVINGS

This is a sweet-and-sour lentil dish that is light but also filling. Serve it with rice or quinoa.

2½ cups water

1 cup dried lentils

1 teaspoon salt

1 to 2 tablespoons olive oil

1 small sweet onion, diced

3 cloves garlic, minced

2 sweet bell or Gypsy peppers, sliced

1 cup chopped fennel bulb

3 tablespoons Marsala wine or unsalted vegetable stock (optional)

2 tablespoons balsamic vinegar

1. Bring the water to a boil in a small saucepan. Add the lentils and ½ teaspoon of the salt. Lower the heat and cook, uncovered, for about 30 minutes, or until the lentils are tender.

2. Heat the oil in another small saucepan. Add the onion, garlic, and the remaining ½ teaspoon of salt. Cook on medium-low heat for about 5 minutes, or until the onion is translucent. Add the peppers, fennel, and Marsala wine, if desired. Cook, uncovered, for about 10 minutes, or until the vegetables are very tender and the wine has evaporated.

3. When the lentils are tender, drain them and mix them with the vegetables. Stir in the balsamic vinegar and serve.

Stuffed Grape Leaves

YIELD: 4 SERVINGS

(24 pieces)

If you have a grapevine growing in your yard (or a friend's yard), you can pick some of the leaves during early summer. Brine them according to the directions in this recipe, and then stuff them. Pick leaves that are about the size of a woman's hand.

5½ cups water

¾ cup short-grain brown rice

1 tablespoon plus 1 teaspoon salt

24 grape leaves, stems removed

2 tablespoons olive oil

1 small onion, diced

3 cloves garlic, minced

1 tablespoon chopped fresh dill, or ½ teaspoon dried dill weed

1 ripe tomato, finely chopped

¼ cup raw sunflower seeds

1. Bring 1½ cups of the water to a boil in a small saucepan. Stir in the rice, return to a boil, lower the heat, cover, and cook for 30 to 40 minutes, until all the water is absorbed.

2. While the rice is cooking, combine the remaining 4 cups of water and 1 tablespoon of the salt in a medium saucepan and bring to a boil. Add the grape leaves, remove from the heat, and let them soak for at least 20 minutes.

3. While the grape leaves are soaking, heat 1 tablespoon of the oil in a small saucepan. Add the onion, garlic, dill, and the remaining 1 teaspoon of salt. Cook on medium-low heat for about 5 minutes, or until the onion is translucent. Add the tomato and cook for about 5 minutes longer, until it breaks down. Remove from the heat. When the rice is ready, add it to this mixture along with the sunflower seeds and mix well.

4. Preheat the oven to 350 degrees F.

5. Lay a grape leaf in front of you with the smooth side facing down and the stem closest to you. Place 1 tablespoon of the rice mixture

in the center of the leaf. Fold the bottom up and the sides toward the center; then continue rolling. Repeat with the remaining leaves and filling.

6. Oil an 8-inch square baking dish and arrange the stuffed leaves in it, close together in a single layer with the seams facing down. Brush them with the remaining oil, cover the pan with foil, and bake them in the oven for about 30 minutes, or until they are soft.

White Beans with Roasted Peppers

YIELD: 4 SERVINGS

You can eat this bean dish cold, as a salad, or hot with pasta, polenta, or rice.

2 red bell peppers

1 tablespoon olive oil

3 cloves garlic, minced

2 cup cooked or canned white beans, drained

½ cup chopped fresh basil

½ teaspoon salt

2 tablespoons balsamic vinegar

1. Preheat the oven to 400 degrees F.

2. Arrange the peppers on a baking sheet and roast them in the oven for about 30 minutes, until they are very soft and their skins are charred. Remove them from the oven and put them in a paper bag for a few minutes (this will make their skins easier to remove). As soon as they are cool enough to handle, peel off their skins using your fingers and slice them into thin strips.

3. Heat the oil in a medium saucepan. Add the garlic and cook on medium-low heat for about 1 minute. Add the beans, roasted peppers, basil, and salt. Cook for 5 or 10 minutes, until the beans are heated through. Remove from the heat and stir in the balsamic vinegar.

Orzo with Fennel and Roasted Cherry Tomatoes

YIELD: 4 SERVINGS

The roasted cherry tomatoes in this recipe are little explosions of flavor, complementing the mellow flavor of the fennel and the smooth texture of the orzo.

½ pound cherry tomatoes

1 cup chopped fennel bulb

6 cloves garlic, unpeeled

2 tablespoons olive oil

1 teaspoon salt

1½ quarts water

1 pound orzo

Freshly ground black pepper

1. Preheat the oven to 400 degrees F.

2. Toss the cherry tomatoes, fennel, and garlic cloves with 1 tablespoon of the oil and ½ teaspoon of the salt. Spread them on a baking sheet, keeping the garlic cloves separate. Roast in the oven for about 20 minutes, or until the fennel starts to brown and the tomatoes start to wilt.

3. While the vegetables are roasting, bring the water to a boil in a medium saucepan, add the orzo, and cook, stirring frequently, for 6 to 8 minutes, or until it is just tender. Drain well, rinse under cold water to quickly cool, then drain again.

4. Squeeze the pulp out of the garlic cloves and mash it with a fork. Mix the roasted garlic with the remaining 1 tablespoon of oil and ½ teaspoon of salt. Add the roasted tomatoes and fennel and toss until evenly combined. Season with pepper to taste.

Roasted Eggplant Pasta Salad

The chunks of roasted eggplant in this salad do a wonderful job of holding the summery flavors of the other ingredients. I prefer orecchiette pasta, which is shaped like little ears, but any kind other than spaghetti or fettuccine will do.

2 medium eggplants
2½ quarts water
1 pound pasta
2 cups cherry tomatoes, cut in half
¼ cup chopped fresh basil
2 to 3 tablespoons olive oil
2 to 3 tablespoons balsamic vinegar
1 teaspoon salt
Freshly ground black pepper

1. Preheat the oven to 400 degrees F.

2. Prick the eggplants all over with a fork. Place them on a baking sheet and roast them in the oven for about 1 hour, or until they are droopy. When they are cool enough to handle, peel them using your fingers and cut them into bite-size pieces.

3. While the eggplant is roasting, boil the water in a medium saucepan. Add the pasta and cook for 8 to 10 minutes, or until it is tender. Drain well, rinse under cold water to quickly cool, then drain again.

4. Combine the pasta with the eggplant, cherry tomatoes, basil, olive oil, vinegar, salt, and pepper to taste and toss gently.

Lentil Tabouli

YIELD: 4 SERVINGS

I designed this recipe for a friend who loves tabouli but avoids wheat. I like it as much as the traditional version.

2 cups cooked lentils, drained
2 ripe tomatoes, chopped
1 cup chopped fresh parsley
2 tablespoons olive oil
2 tablespoons chopped fresh spearmint, or 1 teaspoon dried
1 tablespoon red wine vinegar
1 teaspoon freshly squeezed lemon juice
1 teaspoon salt
Freshly ground black pepper.

Combine all of the ingredients.

Middle Eastern Chickpea Salad

YIELD: 4 SERVINGS

Serve this salad with Stuffed Eggplant (page 78) for a perfect summer meal.

2 cups cooked or canned chickpeas, drained
2 ripe tomatoes, chopped
¼ cup chopped fresh parsley
2 tablespoons olive oil
Juice of ½ lemon
1 tablespoon chopped fresh spearmint, or 1 teaspoon dried
1 teaspoon salt
Freshly ground black pepper

Combine all of the ingredients.

Lentil-Barley Salad with Fresh Fava Beans

YIELD: 4 SERVINGS

Fresh fava beans are pricey, and they are a lot of work because you have to shell them twice, but they are special and in season so briefly that they are well worth the effort. In this salad they are combined with lentils and barley, which are also ancient foods.

5 cups water

½ cup pearl barley

1 pound unshelled fresh fava beans

1 cup cooked or canned lentils, drained

1 cucumber, peeled, cut into quarters lengthwise, and sliced

½ cup chopped fresh parsley

Juice of ½ lemon

1 to 2 tablespoons olive oil

½ teaspoon salt

Freshly ground black pepper

1. Bring 1 cup of the water to a boil in a small saucepan. Stir in the barley, lower the heat, cover, and cook for 20 to 30 minutes, until all of the water is absorbed. Cool the barley quickly by rinsing it under cold water in a fine mesh strainer. Drain it well and shake the strainer to shed the excess water.

2. While the barley is cooking, remove the fava beans from their spongy outer pods. Bring the remaining 4 cups of water to a boil in a small saucepan. Add the shelled beans and cook for 3 minutes. Drain well. Take care not to overcook the beans.

3. When the fava beans are cool enough to handle, gently pierce each pod with a fingernail and carefully squeeze out the bean inside.

4. Mix the fava beans with the barley and all of the remaining ingredients.

Israeli Couscous with Fresh Fava Beans

Israeli couscous is a semolina product that's essentially small round balls of pasta. It has great mouthfeel and is a natural fit with the delicate fresh fava beans in this recipe.

1 pound unshelled fresh fava beans

2 quarts water

1 cup uncooked Israeli couscous

1 cup quartered cherry tomatoes

¼ cup chopped green onions

2 tablespoons chopped fresh parsley

2 tablespoons chopped fresh spearmint

2 tablespoons olive oil

Juice of ½ lemon

½ teaspoon salt

1. Remove the fava beans from their spongy outer pods. Bring 1 quart of the water to a boil in a small saucepan. Add the shelled beans and cook for 3 minutes. Drain well. Take care not to overcook the beans.

2. Bring the remaining 1 quart of water to a boil. Add the couscous and cook for 5 minutes. Drain well in a fine mesh strainer, rinse under cold water to quickly cool it, then drain again.

3. When the fava beans are cool enough to handle, gently pierce each pod with a fingernail and carefully squeeze out the bean inside.

4. Combine the fava beans and couscous with all of the remaining ingredients and mix well.

Israeli Salad

YIELD: 4 SERVINGS

The vegetables in this salad are characteristically chopped into tiny pieces: nothing should be larger than a pea. This makes it delicate and special, almost like a relish. Use a serrated knife for the tomato to cut pieces small enough.

2 cucumbers, finely chopped

1 large ripe tomato, finely chopped

1 green bell pepper, finely chopped

2 tablespoons finely chopped red onion

1 to 2 tablespoons olive oil

1 to 2 tablespoons red wine vinegar

½ teaspoon salt

Freshly ground black pepper

Combine all of the ingredients.

Height-of-the-Season Tomato Salad

YIELD: 4 SERVINGS

Every year I see more colorful heirloom tomatoes at farmers' markets. This recipe shows them off at their simplest and most elegant.

1 pound chopped ripe tomatoes (preferably a colorful variety)

¼ cup chopped fresh basil

2 tablespoons balsamic vinegar

2 tablespoons olive oil

½ teaspoon salt

Combine all of the ingredients. Let stand for about 10 minutes before serving.

Picnic Coleslaw

This is a vegan version of a classic summer slaw. You can shred the cabbage in a food processor or patiently by hand. It's worth taking the extra time to slice the thinnest shreds you possibly can.

½ pound soft tofu

2 tablespoons olive oil

1 tablespoon freshly squeezed lemon juice

1 teaspoon salt

1 head cabbage, finely shredded

1 red onion, finely diced

1 cup peeled and grated carrot

2 tablespoons red wine vinegar

1 tablespoon finely chopped fresh dill, or 1 teaspoon dried dill weed

Freshly ground black pepper

1. Combine the tofu, oil, lemon juice, and ½ teaspoon of the salt in a food processor or blender and process until smooth.

2. Combine the cabbage, onion, and carrot in a large bowl.

3. Pour the tofu mixture into the bowl with the vegetables. Add the vinegar, dill, remaining salt, and pepper to taste and toss until well mixed.

Purslane with Shaved Fennel and Cherry Tomatoes

YIELD: 4 SERVINGS

Purslane has omega-3 fatty acids, which have been linked to cardiovascular health. It has small, spongy leaves that separate easily from their stems.

    1 pint cherry tomatoes, cut into quarters
    1 cup purslane leaves
    1 cup shaved fennel bulb (use a vegetable peeler)
    1 tablespoon olive oil
    1 tablespoon balsamic vinegar
    ½ teaspoon salt
    Freshly ground black pepper

Combine all of the ingredients.

Curried Cucumber Salad

YIELD: 4 SERVINGS

Serve this salad as a cooling accompaniment to curries.

    2 cucumbers, peeled and chopped
    Juice of 1 lime
    2 tablespoons chopped fresh cilantro
    1 tablespoon olive oil
    ½ teaspoon salt
    ½ teaspoon ground cumin
    ½ teaspoon ground coriander
    ½ teaspoon ground turmeric
    ½ teaspoon ground cardamom
    Cayenne

Combine all of the ingredients.

Three Bean Salad

Unlike a traditional three bean salad, which uses canned or dried beans along with fresh green beans, this version uses three different colors of fresh beans. Make sure to cook the purple ones only very briefly; otherwise they will turn green and you'll have two colors rather than three.

¼ pound green beans, trimmed and cut into 1-inch pieces

¼ pound yellow wax beans, trimmed and cut into 1-inch pieces

¼ pound purple pole beans, trimmed and cut into 1-inch pieces

1 ripe tomato, finely chopped

2 tablespoons chopped fresh chives

1 tablespoon olive oil

1 tablespoon balsamic vinegar

½ teaspoon salt

Freshly ground black pepper

1. Steam the green and yellow beans for 2 to 3 minutes. Then add the purple beans and steam for 1 minute longer.

2. Mix the steamed beans with all of the remaining ingredients.

Blueberry Bars

YIELD: 8 OR 10 BARS

These tasty, easy bars feature blueberry compote on an oat and flour crust. You can wrap them and take them anywhere.

½ cup nonhydrogenated margarine, softened

¾ cup unrefined cane sugar

1¾ cups unbleached white or whole wheat flour

½ teaspoon baking soda

¼ teaspoon salt

1 cup rolled oats

½ cup fruit juice (any kind except citrus)

1 pint blueberries

1 teaspoon vanilla extract

1 tablespoon white or brown rice flour

1. Preheat the oven to 375 degrees F.

2. Combine the margarine and sugar in a small bowl. Sift together the wheat flour, baking soda, and salt. Add the sugar and margarine and mix well. Add the oats, mixing them in with your hands. The mixture should be crumbly but hold together when squeezed.

3. For the crust, spread two-thirds of the oat mixture on the bottom of an 8-inch square baking pan, pressing it down firmly. Set aside the remaining oat mixture. Bake the crust for about 20 minutes, or until it is set.

4. While the crust is baking, heat the juice gently in a medium saucepan. Add the blueberries and vanilla extract and cook for about 10 minutes, or until the berries break down. Sprinkle in the rice flour, stirring constantly until the mixture thickens.

5. Spread the blueberry mixture over the crust and sprinkle the reserved oat mixture on top. Bake for about 10 minutes, or until the topping starts to brown.

Peach-Pecan Cake

This dense, fruity cake uses the classic Southern combination of peaches and pecans. It makes a fine breakfast or a worthy dessert.

2 ripe peaches, chopped into bite-size pieces
½ cup nonhydrogenated margarine, softened
1 cup unrefined cane sugar
2 cups unbleached white or whole wheat flour
½ teaspoon salt
½ teaspoon baking soda
⅔ cup chopped pecans

1. Preheat the oven to 375 degrees F. Oil an 8-inch square baking pan.

2. Mix the peaches with the margarine. Then stir in the sugar.

3. Sift together the flour, salt, and baking soda. Stir the flour mixture into the peach mixture. Then stir in the pecans.

4. Pour into the prepared baking pan. Bake for 30 to 40 minutes, or until the top is golden brown and a knife inserted into the center comes out clean.

Raspberry-Almond Cake

YIELD: 8 OR 10 PIECES

This cake takes on the deep red color of raspberries, as well as their incomparable flavor

  2 cups raspberries

  ½ cup nonhydrogenated margarine, softened

  1 cup unrefined cane sugar

  2 cups unbleached white or whole wheat flour

  ½ teaspoon salt

  ½ teaspoon baking soda

  ⅔ cup sliced almonds

1. Preheat the oven to 375 degrees F. Oil an 8-inch square baking pan.

2. Mix the raspberries with the margarine. Then stir in the sugar.

3. Sift together the flour, salt, and baking soda. Stir the flour mixture into the raspberry mixture. Then stir in the almonds.

4. Pour into the prepared baking pan. Bake for 30 to 40 minutes, or until the top is golden brown and a knife inserted into the center comes out clean.

Mixed Berry Compote

YIELD: ABOUT 3 CUPS

You can serve this tasty fruit sauce warm or chilled with pancakes or over nondairy ice cream. It also freezes well, so you can save a taste of summer for later in the year.

> 1 cup fruit juice (any kind except citrus)
> 1 cup blueberries
> 1 cup raspberries
> 1 cup chopped strawberries
> 1 tablespoon sweetener of your choice
> 1 teaspoon vanilla extract
> 1 tablespoon white or brown rice flour

1. Gently heat the juice in a medium saucepan. Add the blueberries, raspberries, strawberries, and sweetener. Cook on medium-low heat, stirring occasionally, for 10 to 15 minutes, until the berries break down. Stir in the vanilla extract.

2. Sprinkle in the rice flour, stirring constantly until the mixture thickens.

Caramelized Apricots with Hazelnuts

YIELD: 4 SERVINGS

Searing apricots releases their sugars, giving them a tasty coating. Here the soft, ripe fruit is served with crunchy toasted hazelnuts. You can substitute any kind of nut, ideally one that grows in your area.

1 tablespoon canola oil

4 apricots, cut in half, pits removed

½ cup chopped hazelnuts or other nuts of your choice

1. Heat the oil in a medium skillet. Arrange as many of the apricot halves as you can fit in the pan, with their flat sides facing down. Cook for about 5 minutes, or until the surfaces touching the pan start to brown. Cook them in several batches if you can't fit them in all at once.

2. While the apricots are cooking, preheat the oven to 375 degrees F. Spread the hazelnuts in a single layer on a baking sheet and roast them in the oven for 2 to 3 minutes, or until they are aromatic.

3. Sprinkle the toasted hazelnuts over the apricot halves and serve.

Nectarine and Blueberry Cobbler

YIELD: 8 SERVINGS

If you have perfectly ripe fruit for this recipe, you won't need any sugar in the fruity base, just a little in the biscuit top crust. If you own a good-quality saucepan, one with a thick bottom, use it for the fruit so it can heat slowly and evenly. Unbleached white flour makes a lighter, fluffier biscuit. Whole wheat flour makes a denser, more healthful topping.

4 ripe nectarines, diced

1 pint blueberries

3 cups unbleached white or whole wheat flour, or a mixture

1 tablespoon unrefined cane sugar

2 teaspoons baking powder

½ teaspoon salt

1 cup nonhydrogenated margarine, softened

1 cup water

1. Preheat the oven to 375 degrees F.

2. Combine the nectarines and blueberries in a saucepan. Heat them gently over medium-low heat, stirring often, for about 5 minutes, or until the nectarines release their juice. If the mixture seems too dry, add 1 to 3 tablespoons of water.

3. To make the biscuit dough, combine the flour, sugar, baking powder, and salt in a medium bowl. Mix in the margarine using a fork or your fingers. Stir in the water and mix until smooth.

4. Spread the fruit mixture in the bottom of an 8-inch square pan. Spoon the biscuit dough on top, spreading it as evenly as you can. It's okay if there are gaps.

5. Bake for 30 to 40 minutes, or until the biscuit topping starts to brown.

Fall

3

Early fall is my favorite time to eat, because we still have access to all of the great summer produce along with the early cold-weather crops. It's the time for hayrides and harvest festivals, with colorful and abundant produce and temperatures still warm enough to party outdoors. We welcome the first cool days after the heat of summer, taking comfort in hearty soups and dense, satisfying winter squash. Fall holidays celebrate seasonal foods, with pumpkins for Halloween and potatoes, yams, and cranberries for Thanksgiving. The farmers' markets wind down, but before they go they offer us foods that will last a while, cool weather fruits and vegetables with ample shelf life to feed us during the days ahead.

Fall Produce

EARLY FALL	MID-FALL	LATE FALL
bell peppers	apples	broccoli
chiles	chanterelle mushrooms	cabbage
cilantro	collard greens	cauliflower
fennel	cranberry beans	cranberries
Swiss chard	kohlrabi	parsnips
tomatillos	pickling cucumbers	pears
winter squash	plums	yams

Squash Hummus

This recipe is a unique twist on a traditional favorite. Serve it with chips or pita bread, or spread it on sandwiches.

1 acorn squash
¼ cup tahini
Juice of 1 lemon
2 tablespoons olive oil

1 tablespoon dried parsley flakes
1 clove garlic, minced
½ teaspoon salt

1. Cut the squash in half lengthwise and remove the seeds. Cut the halves into chunks that will fit in your vegetable steamer and steam them for 20 to 30 minutes, or until they are very soft.

2. Scoop out the pulp and transfer it to a food processor. Add the remaining ingredients and process until smooth.

Cilantro-Lime Dressing

Use this dressing if you are serving a salad with a Mexican meal. Alternatively, use it to marinate cucumber, cabbage, or tomatoes.

⅓ cup olive oil
⅓ cup red wine vinegar
¼ cup chopped fresh cilantro
Juice of 1 lime
1 teaspoon chili powder (mild or hot)
½ teaspoon ground cumin
½ teaspoon dried oregano
½ teaspoon salt

Whisk together all of the ingredients.

Pepperonata

YIELD: ABOUT 3 CUPS

This is a flavorful tomato sauce made with a variety of colorful sweet peppers. Serve it over pasta or polenta.

1 tablespoon olive oil

1 medium onion, chopped

3 cloves garlic, minced

1 teaspoon salt

4 bell peppers, sliced (preferably a combination of red, green, and yellow)

4 ripe tomatoes, cut into bite-size pieces

½ cup chopped fresh basil

Freshly ground black pepper

1. Heat the olive oil in a medium saucepan. Add the onion, garlic, and salt. Cook on medium-low heat for about 5 minutes, or until the onion is translucent.

2. Add the bell peppers and cook, stirring occasionally, for 5 to 10 minutes, until they are tender.

3. Add the tomatoes, basil, and pepper to taste and cook on medium heat, stirring often, for about 10 minutes, or until the tomatoes break down.

Roasted Tomato Salsa

YIELD: ABOUT 3 CUPS

Use very ripe tomatoes for this recipe. Some farmers' market vendors will be more than happy to sell you their seconds cheaply.

> 4 ripe tomatoes
> 3 mild chiles (Anaheim or poblano; see note)
> 1 hot chile (jalapeño or cayenne; see note)
> 1 teaspoon olive oil
> ¼ cup chopped fresh cilantro
> 1 tablespoon red wine vinegar
> ½ teaspoon salt

1. Preheat the oven to 400 degrees F.
2. Using your hands, rub the tomatoes and chiles with the oil. Arrange them on a baking sheet and roast them in the oven for 45 to 60 minutes, or until the skins soften and turn brown.
3. When they are cool enough to handle, remove the stems from the chiles and the cores from the tops of the tomatoes. Transfer them to a food processor or blender and add the cilantro, vinegar, and salt. Process until coarsely chopped and well combined.

NOTE: I use both mild and hot chiles in this recipe. It doesn't take many hot ones to make a spicy salsa, and the mild ones add extra flavor. If you like your salsa really spicy, use more of the hot ones; if you like it milder, you can leave out the hot ones altogether.

Roasted Tomatillo Salsa

YIELD: ABOUT 2 CUPS

Tomatillos are a different species from tomatoes. Unlike unripe green tomatoes, they have a papery skin that needs to be removed. They are tart and flavorful and make a lovely salsa.

- 1 pound tomatillos, papery outer skins removed
- 1 pasilla, poblano, or Anaheim chile
- 1 jalapeño chile
- 1 teaspoon olive oil
- ¼ cup chopped fresh cilantro
- 2 tablespoons red wine vinegar
- ½ teaspoon salt

1. Preheat the oven to 400 degrees F.

2. Using your hands, rub the tomatillos and chiles with the oil. Arrange them on a baking sheet and roast them in the oven for 45 to 60 minutes, or until the chiles turn brown and droop.

3. When they are cool enough to handle, remove the stems from the chiles and the cores from the tops of the tomatillos. Transfer them to a blender or food processor, add the cilantro, vinegar, and salt, and process until well combined but still a little chunky.

Roasted Chile Paste

YIELD: ABOUT 1 CUP

This recipe makes a spicy condiment that's great with Mexican or Asian foods. It will keep in the refrigerator for at least two weeks.

1 pound chiles (mild, hot, or a mixture, depending on your preference)

1 teaspoon olive oil
2 tablespoons red wine vinegar
1 teaspoon salt

1. Preheat the oven to 400 degrees F.
2. Using your hands, rub the chiles with the oil. Arrange them on a baking sheet and roast them in the oven for 45 to 60 minutes, or until they begin to brown.
3. When the chiles are cool enough to handle, remove the stems and place the chiles in a food processor or blender. Add the vinegar and salt and process until smooth.

Pico de Gallo

YIELD: ABOUT 2 CUPS

This recipe uses almost exactly the same ingredients as the Roasted Tomato Salsa (page 104), but it has a very different flavor and texture. I like to keep some of each on hand.

3 ripe tomatoes, very finely diced
1 pasilla, poblano, or Anaheim chile, very finely diced
1 jalapeño or serrano chile, very finely diced (optional)
¼ cup chopped fresh cilantro
1 to 2 tablespoons red wine vinegar
½ teaspoon salt

Combine all of the ingredients.

Squash, Parsnip, and Fennel Bruschetta

YIELD: 20 TO 25 SLICES

This recipe makes a colorful appetizer. The vegetables are so flavorful they need almost no seasoning.

1 delicata squash

1 small fennel bulb

1 medium parsnip

½ teaspoon salt

1 baguette (day-old bread is fine)

2 to 3 tablespoons olive oil

1. Cut the squash in half lengthwise and remove the seeds. Trim the top and bottom of the fennel, slice it in half lengthwise, cut out the core, and chop it into 1-inch pieces. Peel the parsnip, trim the top and bottom, and cut it into 2-inch chunks.

2. Arrange the vegetables in a steamer basket and steam them for about 20 minutes, until the squash and parsnip are soft.

3. Scoop the squash out of its skin and transfer the pulp to a food processor along with the fennel, parsnip, and salt and process until smooth.

4. Preheat the oven to 350 degrees F. Cut the baguette into slices about ⅔ inch thick. Brush the slices with the oil (a pastry brush will make this easier) and toast them in the oven for 4 to 5 minutes, until they are a little crispy on top but not hard all the way through. (You can put the slices on a baking sheet or directly on the oven rack.)

5. Place about 1 teaspoon of the vegetable mixture on top of 1 slice of the bread and spread it to form a thin layer. Repeat with the remaining bread and vegetable mixture.

Veggie-Walnut Pinwheels

These savory rolls are portable, and they make a great snack or appetizer. This recipe makes quite a few, so you can freeze some if you are not going to eat them all right away. You can use unbleached white or whole wheat flour, or any combination you prefer. White flour makes a lighter dough, while whole wheat flour makes a denser pastry but has more nutrients.

DOUGH

1 tablespoon active dry yeast

1½ cups warm water

3 tablespoons olive oil

1 teaspoon salt

4½ cups unbleached white or whole wheat flour, or a combination

FILLING

1 medium yam, peeled and cut into chunks

1 cup broccoli florets

1 cup cauliflower florets

½ cup walnuts

4 button mushrooms

2 shallots

4 cloves garlic, peeled

3 tablespoons olive oil

2 tablespoons chopped fresh basil, or 1 teaspoon dried

½ teaspoon salt

1 tablespoon balsamic vinegar

1. To make the dough, dissolve the yeast in the warm water. Add the olive oil and salt. Mix in the flour and knead the dough for a few minutes on a floured surface, adding more flour if it sticks. Set the dough aside in a warm place to rise for 30 to 40 minutes.

2. Preheat the oven to 375 degrees F. Oil 2 baking sheets.

3. While the dough is rising, prepare the filling. Steam the yam for 10 to 15 minutes, or until it is soft enough to mash. Pulse the broccoli, cauliflower, walnuts, mushrooms, shallots, and garlic in a food

processor until they are finely chopped. If your food processor is small, chop the them in batches.

4. Heat the olive oil in a medium saucepan. Add the chopped vegetables and walnuts along with the basil and salt. Cook on medium-low heat for about 5 minutes. Add the mashed yam and the balsamic vinegar and mix well.

5. Divide the dough in half. Roll out each half on a floured surface to make a rectangle about 6 inches wide and 12 inches long. Spread half of the vegetable mixture on each piece, leaving a 1-inch margin all the way around. Roll from left to right. Trim the tops and bottoms and cut each roll into 10 pieces. Arrange the pieces on the prepared baking sheets, cut side up, and flatten each pinwheel a bit with your hand. Brush them with olive oil and bake for 20 to 30 minutes, or until they start to brown.

Roasted Pumpkin Seeds

YIELD: 2 CUPS

Don't throw out those seeds when you scoop them out of your pumpkin. Season and roast them for a spicy, portable snack.

2 cups cleaned pumpkin seeds
2 teaspoons olive oil
1 teaspoon chili powder (mild or hot)
½ teaspoon ground cumin
½ teaspoon dried oregano
½ teaspoon salt

1. Preheat the oven to 400 degrees F.

2. Toss all of the ingredients together until the pumpkin seeds are evenly coated. Spread them in a thin layer on a baking sheet and roast them in the oven for 15 to 20 minutes, until they start to brown.

Parsnip and Fennel Soup

YIELD: 4 SERVINGS

This puréed soup is a wonderful Thanksgiving offering.

4 cups unsalted vegetable stock or water
3 parsnips, peeled and cut into chunks
1 medium onion, peeled and quartered
1 cup chopped fennel bulb
6 cloves garlic, peeled
1 teaspoon salt
½ teaspoon whole fennel seeds
Freshly ground black pepper

1. Bring the stock to a boil in a medium saucepan. Add the parsnips, onion, fennel, garlic, salt, fennel seeds, and pepper to taste. Bring back to a boil, lower the heat, and cook for 30 to 40 minutes, until the vegetables are very tender.

2. Strain the soup and set aside the stock. Process the vegetables in batches in a blender until smooth, adding some of the stock as needed. Combine the blended vegetables with the remaining stock. Taste and add additional salt, if needed. Reheat the soup, if necessary, before serving.

Harvest Corn and Squash Soup

YIELD: 6 SERVINGS

Make this soup during late September or early October, when winter squash season overlaps with the last of the tomatoes, chiles, and corn. It's a hearty soup that makes the best of the produce of both seasons.

1 acorn or kabocha squash

2 tablespoons olive oil

1 medium onion, chopped

2 pasilla, poblano, or Anaheim chiles, diced

1 jalapeño chile, diced (optional)

4 cloves garlic, minced

1 tablespoon chili powder (mild or hot)

1 teaspoon salt

1 teaspoon ground cumin

1 teaspoon dried oregano

4 cups unsalted vegetable stock or water

2 ripe tomatoes, coarsely chopped

1 cup fresh corn kernels (2 to 3 ears)

½ cup chopped fresh cilantro

1. Cut the squash in half lengthwise and remove the seeds. Cut the halves into chunks that will fit in your vegetable steamer and steam them for 20 to 30 minutes, or until they are very soft.

2. While the squash is steaming, heat the oil in a medium soup pot. Add the onion, chiles, garlic, chili powder, salt, cumin, and oregano. Cook on medium-low heat for about 10 minutes, until the onion and chiles are tender.

3. Add the stock, tomatoes, corn, and cilantro and bring to a boil. Cook on medium-low heat for about 20 minutes, until the tomatoes start to break down.

4. When the squash is soft, remove it from the steamer. When it is cool enough to handle, scoop out the pulp and mash it with a fork, spoon, or potato masher. Stir the pulp into the soup and mix well. Taste and add additional salt, if needed, and serve.

Caribbean Pumpkin-Coconut Soup

YIELD: 6 SERVINGS

This is a thick, creamy, spicy soup. It uses the bounty of fall, but makes me think of sunshine.

2 pounds kabocha pumpkin or winter squash

2 quarts unsalted vegetable stock or water

2 leeks, cut in half lengthwise, cleaned well, and chopped

2 chiles (mild or hot), diced

2 tablespoons grated fresh ginger

4 cloves garlic, minced

1 teaspoon salt

1 bunch collard greens (4 to 6 leaves), cut into thin strips

1 can (14 ounces) coconut milk

Juice of 1 lime

1 teaspoon fresh thyme, or 1/2 teaspoon dried

½ teaspoon ground allspice

1. Cut the pumpkin in half top to bottom and remove the seeds. Cut the halves into chunks that will fit in your vegetable steamer and steam them for 20 to 30 minutes, or until they are very soft.

2. Bring the stock to a boil in a medium soup pot. Add the leeks, chiles, ginger, garlic, and salt. Cook on medium-low heat for about 30 minutes. Add the collard greens and cook for 15 to 20 minutes, stirring occasionally.

3. Scoop out the squash pulp, place it in a blender or food processor, and process until smooth. Add a small amount of the stock, as needed, to facilitate processing. Combine the blended squash with the rest of the soup. Stir in the coconut milk, lime juice, thyme, and allspice. Taste and add additional salt, if needed. Cook for about 5 minutes longer, until heated through, and serve.

Greek Vegetable Soup with Orzo

The orzo pasta in this soup makes it filling, but the fresh dill and mint make the flavors surprisingly light.

1 tablespoon olive oil

1 medium onion, diced

4 cloves garlic, chopped

2 cups broccoli florets

2 carrots, peeled (if desired) and sliced

2 stalks celery, sliced

2 tablespoons finely chopped fresh dill

1 tablespoon finely chopped fresh spearmint

1 teaspoon salt

6 ripe tomatoes, diced

1 quart water

½ cup orzo

1. Heat the oil in a medium saucepan. Add the onion and garlic and cook on medium-low heat for about 5 minutes, until the onion is translucent. Add the broccoli, carrots, celery, dill, spearmint, and salt and cook for 5 minutes.

2. Add the tomatoes and cook for 10 to 15 minutes, until they start to break down. Lower the heat to medium-low and cook for 10 minutes longer.

3. While the soup is cooking, boil the water in a small saucepan. Add the orzo and cook, stirring often, for about 10 minutes. Drain the orzo and add it to the soup. Taste and add additional salt, if needed. Simmer for 5 minutes and serve.

Couscous and Roasted Pepper Soup

YIELD: 6 SERVINGS

This thick soup has Middle Eastern flavors as well as couscous, a yellow semolina pasta that adds a colorful complement to the roasted red peppers.

3 red bell peppers

6 cups unsalted vegetable stock

1 small or medium butternut squash, peeled and cut into 1-inch cubes

1 medium onion, chopped

1 tablespoon ground cumin

1 teaspoon salt

2 cloves garlic, minced

⅓ cup uncooked couscous

Juice of 1 lemon

1. Preheat the oven to 400 degrees F.

2. Arrange the peppers on a baking sheet and roast them in the oven for about 30 minutes, until they are very soft and their skins are charred. Remove them from the oven and put them in a paper bag for a few minutes (this will make their skins easier to remove). As soon as they are cool enough to handle, peel off their skins using your fingers and slice them into thin strips.

3. While the peppers are roasting, combine the stock, squash, onion, cumin, salt, and garlic in a medium soup pot. Cook on medium heat for about 30 minutes, stirring occasionally.

4. Add the couscous and roasted pepper strips and cover the pot. Remove from the heat and let sit for about 5 minutes, until the couscous is soft.

5. Stir in the lemon juice. Taste and add additional salt, if needed, and serve.

French Tomato Soup

YIELD: 6 SERVINGS

Basil, fennel, and orange juice give this soup a light and unusual flavor.

1 tablespoon olive oil

1 medium onion, chopped

1 fennel bulb, trimmed and finely chopped

2 to 3 cloves garlic, minced

1 teaspoon salt

8 ripe tomatoes, chopped

¼ cup chopped fresh basil

⅔ cup orange juice

1. Heat the oil in a medium saucepan. Add the onion, fennel, garlic, and salt. Cook for about 10 minutes, stirring occasionally, until the fennel is soft and the onion is translucent.

2. Add the tomatoes and basil. Cook on medium heat, stirring occasionally, for about 15 minutes, until the tomatoes break down.

3. Stir in the orange juice and serve.

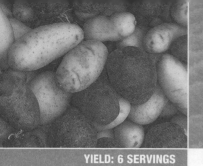

Twice-Roasted Potatoes

Yukon Gold potatoes are especially lovely in this recipe.

3 medium potatoes (any kind but russets)
1 tablespoon olive oil
2 cloves garlic, minced
½ teaspoon dried dill weed
Pinch of salt

1. Preheat the oven to 400 degrees F. Place the potatoes directly on the oven rack and bake them for about 45 minutes, or until they are soft.

2. When the potatoes are nearly ready, heat the oil in a small saucepan. Cook the garlic for about 30 seconds, just until you can smell it. Remove it from the heat and stir in the dill weed and salt.

3. When the potatoes are cool enough to handle, slice them in half and spread the garlic mixture over the cut surfaces.

4. Arrange the potatoes on a baking sheet, cut side up, and bake them for 10 to 15 minutes, or until they start to brown.

Greek Greens

YIELD: 6 SERVINGS

Dill and fennel spice these tender greens.

1 tablespoon olive oil

1 medium onion, chopped

1 fennel bulb, trimmed and chopped

2 cloves garlic, minced

½ teaspoon salt

1 bunch spinach (about ½ pound), chopped

1 bunch red chard (4 to 6 leaves), chopped

1 bunch collard greens (4 to 6 leaves), chopped

1 tablespoon chopped fresh dill, or 1 teaspoon dried dill weed

Juice of ½ lemon

1. Heat the oil in a large saucepan. Add the onion, fennel, garlic, and salt. Cook for about 10 minutes, or until the fennel is soft and the onion is translucent.

2. Add the spinach, chard, and collard greens, a handful at a time, adding more as they cook down. When all of the greens are tender, stir in the dill and lemon juice and cook for 1 minute longer.

Brazilian Collard Greens

YIELD: 4 SERVINGS

The collard greens in this dish should be almost shaved, like coleslaw. If you like, serve them sprinkled with manioc flour, a crunchy topping used in traditional Brazilian food; it is usually available in Latin grocery stores.

2 tablespoons olive oil

6 cloves garlic, minced

2 bunches collard greens (4 to 6 leaves per bunch), cut into ⅛-inch strips

½ teaspoon salt

1. Heat the oil in a medium saucepan. Add the garlic and cook on low heat for 1 minute.

2. Add the collard greens and salt. Cook, stirring often, for about 10 minutes, or until the greens are tender.

Chard and Chanterelles in Wine Sauce

YIELD: 4 SERVINGS

This recipe uses some of the most special and underused members of the onion family: leeks and shallots. The white wine sauce carries their flavors gracefully.

1 tablespoon olive oil

2 leeks, cut in half lengthwise, cleaned well, and chopped

3 shallots, thinly sliced

2 cloves garlic, minced

½ pound chanterelle mushrooms, sliced

¼ cup white wine or a nonalcoholic substitute

1 bunch chard (4 to 6 leaves), stems removed and chopped

1 teaspoon salt

1. Heat the oil in a medium saucepan. Add the leeks, shallots, and garlic and cook, stirring occasionally, for about 5 minutes.

2. Add the mushrooms and wine and cook for about 5 minutes, until the mushrooms start to release their juice.

3. Add the chard and salt and cook, stirring occasionally, until the chard is tender, about 5 minutes.

Velvety Squash with Roasted Garlic

YIELD: 4 SERVINGS

I think of this satisfying comfort food as a grown-up form of mashed potatoes (but kids enjoy it too).

1 acorn squash

4 cloves garlic, unpeeled

½ teaspoon olive oil

1 tablespoon balsamic vinegar

½ teaspoon salt

1. Cut the squash in half lengthwise and remove the seeds. Cut the halves into chunks that will fit in your vegetable steamer and steam them for 20 to 30 minutes, or until they are very soft.

2. While the squash is steaming, preheat the oven to 400 degrees F. Rub the garlic cloves with the oil. Wrap them in foil and roast them in the oven for 25 to 35 minutes, or until they are soft enough that you can squeeze the pulp out of the skins.

3. When the squash is ready, scoop out the pulp into a bowl and mash it well with a fork or potato masher. Squeeze the garlic pulp directly into the squash. Add the balsamic vinegar and salt and mix well.

Braised Carrots with Cranberries

YIELD: 4 SERVINGS

Here's a sweet-and-sour vegetable dish with a deep, mellow flavor. You can use the extra braising liquid as a sauce with any kind of grain or with potatoes.

2 tablespoons olive oil

4 cloves garlic, minced

¼ cup orange juice

2 tablespoons balsamic vinegar

1 teaspoon chopped fresh rosemary

½ teaspoon salt

2 cups peeled and sliced carrots

½ cup cranberries

1. Heat the oil gently in a medium saucepan. Add the garlic and cook on low heat for about 1 minute. Add the orange juice, vinegar, rosemary, and salt.

2. Bring the mixture to a boil. Add the carrots and cranberries. Lower the heat, cover, and simmer for about 15 minutes, or until the carrots are tender.

Masa Patties with Nuts and Vegetables

The ancient inhabitants of Mexico discovered that they could significantly enhance the nutritional value of corn by mixing it with something alkaline, such as ash or ground limestone. Masa harina is corn flour that has been treated in this fashion. In addition to adding nutrients, this process also changes the taste. These patties show off the rich flavor of the masa harina, which is mixed with nuts and vegetables and then panfried. Serve them with black beans and your favorite salsa.

2 tablespoons olive oil

1 medium zucchini, chopped into pea-size pieces

1 small onion, diced

1 pasilla, poblano, or Anaheim chile, diced

1 teaspoon salt

1 teaspoon chili powder (mild or hot)

½ teaspoon ground cumin

½ teaspoon dried oregano

¼ cup slivered almonds

2 cups water

2 cups masa harina

2 to 3 tablespoons canola oil

1. Heat 1 tablespoon of the olive oil in a medium saucepan. Add the zucchini, onion, chile, ½ teaspoon of the salt, and all of the chili powder, cumin, and oregano. Cook on medium-low heat for about 5 minutes, or until the onion is translucent. Remove from the heat and stir in the almonds.

2. In a separate saucepan, combine the water with the remaining 1 tablespoon of olive oil and ½ teaspoon of salt and bring to a boil. Remove from the heat and quickly stir in the masa harina and the vegetable mixture. Mix well. When the mixture is just cool enough to handle, form it into 10 balls with your hands, or use an ice cream scoop. Flatten the balls to form patties.

3. Heat the canola oil in a medium skillet. Cook the patties a few at a time, flipping them so they brown on both sides.

Wild Rice Pilaf

YIELD: 6 SERVINGS

This recipe makes a tasty Thanksgiving side dish.

    5 cups water
    1 cup wild rice
    1 cup short-grain brown rice
    1 to 2 tablespoons olive oil
    1 leek, cut in half lengthwise, cleaned well, and chopped
    1 carrot, peeled (if desired) and finely diced
    2 to 3 shallots, diced
    1 teaspoons salt
    2 cloves garlic, minced
    ½ cup chopped fresh parsley
    ½ cup raw sunflower seeds

1. Bring the water to a boil in a large saucepan. Add the wild rice. Cover and cook on medium heat for about 30 minutes. Add the brown rice and bring the liquid back to a boil. Then lower the heat, cover, and continue cooking for about 45 minutes, or until all of the water is absorbed.

2. While the rice is cooking, heat the olive oil in a medium saucepan. Add the leek, carrot, shallots, salt, and garlic. Cook on medium-low heat, stirring occasionally, for 10 to 15 minutes, until all of the vegetables are tender. Add the parsley and sunflower seeds and cook for 1 minute longer.

3. When the rice is ready, mix it with the vegetables. Taste and add additional salt, if needed, and serve.

Wild Rice with Cranberries

YIELD: 4 SERVINGS

Here's another Thanksgiving dish that brings together a wealth of seasonal flavors.

2½ cups water

½ cup wild rice

⅔ cup cranberries

½ cup brown rice

1 teaspoon finely chopped fresh rosemary

1 teaspoon salt

¼ cup orange juice

¼ cup chopped walnuts

2 tablespoons olive oil

Freshly ground black pepper

1. Bring the water to a boil in a medium saucepan. Add the wild rice, cover, and cook for 30 minutes on medium-low heat.

2. Add the cranberries, brown rice, rosemary, and salt. Cook, covered, for about 45 minutes, or until all of the liquid is absorbed.

3. Remove from the heat and stir in the orange juice, walnuts, oil, and pepper to taste.

Pumpkin Seed Stuffing

My version of this traditional Thanksgiving favorite stars roasted pumpkin seeds, a seasonal fall food.

1 tablespoon olive oil

4 stalks celery, diced

1 medium onion, finely chopped

½ cup chopped fresh parsley

1 tablespoon chopped fresh sage, or 1 teaspoon dried

½ teaspoon salt

Freshly ground black pepper

1 loaf hard-crusted bread, cut into 1-inch cubes

1 cup unsalted vegetable stock

1 cup Roasted Pumpkin Seeds (page 109)

1. Preheat the oven to 375 degrees F.

2. Heat the oil in a medium saucepan. Add the celery, onion, parsley, sage, salt, and pepper to taste. Cook on medium heat, stirring often, for 5 to 10 minutes, or until the onion is translucent.

3. Transfer the onion mixture to a large bowl and add the bread cubes, vegetable stock, and pumpkins seeds. Mix well.

4. Spread the mixture on a baking sheet and bake for 20 to 30 minutes, or until the bread is crusty and brown.

Acorn Squash
and Wild Rice Patties

YIELD: 6 PATTIES

These delicate, satisfying patties will make a wonderful addition to your Thanksgiving spread. Serve them with your favorite mushroom gravy.

1 acorn squash
2½ cups water
½ cup wild rice
½ cup brown rice
¼ cup olive oil
½ cup chopped onion
¼ cup chopped fresh parsley
3 cloves garlic, minced
1 teaspoon salt

1. Cut the squash in half lengthwise and remove the seeds. Cut the halves into chunks that will fit in your vegetable steamer and steam them for 20 to 30 minutes, or until they are very soft.

2. While the squash is steaming, bring the water to a boil in a medium saucepan. Add the wild rice, cover, and cook on medium-low heat for about 30 minutes. Add the brown rice and cook for 30 to 45 minutes, or until all of the water is absorbed.

3. Heat 2 tablespoons of the oil in a separate small saucepan. Add the onion, parsley, garlic, and salt. Cook on medium-low heat for about 5 minutes, or until the onion is translucent.

4. When the squash is ready, scoop out the pulp into a bowl. Add the rice mixture and the onion mixture and stir until well combined. Shape the mixture into patties.

5. Heat the remaining 2 tablespoons of oil in a medium skillet. Cook the patties for 3 to 5 minutes on each side, or until they start to brown.

NOTE: The patties may be baked instead of panfried, if you prefer. Preheat the oven to 375 degrees F and lightly oil a baking sheet. Arrange the patties on the prepared baking sheet, brush them with a little oil, and bake them for about 20 minutes.

Mexican Roasted Vegetables

YIELD: 4 SERVINGS

You can serve these roasted vegetables as a side dish with any Mexican meal, or you can incorporate them into burritos, enchiladas, tacos, or tamales.

1 quart water

2 medium potatoes (any kind but russets), diced

1 medium red onion, cut in half and sliced

1 medium yellow onion, cut in half and sliced

1 green bell pepper, sliced

1 red or yellow bell pepper, sliced

1 cup sliced button mushrooms

2 carrots, peeled (if desired) and sliced

1 zucchini, sliced

2 tablespoons olive oil

1 teaspoon salt

1 teaspoon chili powder (mild or hot)

½ teaspoon ground cumin

½ teaspoon dried oregano

1. Preheat the oven to 400 degrees F.

2. Bring the water to a boil in a medium saucepan. Parboil the potatoes for about 2 minutes; then drain them well.

3. Toss the potatoes with all of the remaining ingredients. Arrange the seasoned vegetables on a baking sheet and roast them in the oven for 30 to 40 minutes, or until they start to brown.

Pickled Peppers

These peppers have a wonderful balance of sweet-and-sour flavors. You can serve them mixed with pasta, as a relish, or on top of a green salad. If you are using hot peppers, you can also serve them with rice and beans. Use a variety of colors for an attractive mix.

2 tablespoons olive oil

1 medium onion, chopped

3 cloves garlic, minced

4 medium peppers, cut into strips (use sweet peppers or a mixture of sweet and hot)

½ teaspoon salt

3 tablespoons red wine vinegar

1. Heat the oil in a medium saucepan. Add the onion and garlic. Cook on medium-low heat for about 5 minutes, or until the onion is translucent.

2. Add the peppers and salt. Cook for about 5 minutes, until the peppers are soft.

3. Stir in the vinegar and cook for 1 to 2 minutes longer.

Pickled Carrots and Jalapeño Chiles

YIELD: ABOUT 2 CUPS

You can use this relish in burritos or enchiladas. It will keep in the refrigerator for several weeks.

    1 tablespoon olive oil
    1 medium onion, diced
    3 cloves garlic, minced
    3 carrots, peeled (if desired) and sliced
    12 to 15 jalapeño chiles, sliced
    ½ cup water
    ¼ cup white vinegar
    1 teaspoon salt

1. Heat the olive oil in a medium saucepan. Add the onion and garlic and cook on medium-low heat for about 5 minutes, or until the onion is translucent.

2. Add all of the remaining ingredients and bring the mixture to a boil. Lower the heat and cook, stirring occasionally, for about 10 minutes.

NOTE: If you wear contact lenses, make sure to wear gloves when you handle the chiles.

Simple Black Beans

Serve this simple, tasty bean dish in burritos, enchiladas, or tacos, or on its own with rice and salsa.

1 tablespoon olive oil

4 cloves garlic, minced

1 pasilla, poblano, or Anaheim chile, diced

1 jalapeño chile, diced (optional)

1 teaspoon chili powder (mild or hot)

½ teaspoon ground cumin

½ teaspoon dried oregano

½ teaspoon salt

2 cups cooked or canned black beans, drained

1. Heat the oil in a small saucepan. Add the garlic, chile(s), chili powder, cumin, oregano, and salt. Cook on medium-low heat for about 5 minutes, or until the chiles are soft.

2. Add the beans and cook for about 5 minutes, until they are heated through.

Pasta with Collard Greens

YIELD: 4 SERVINGS

This is a very simple recipe, but it's one of my favorite meals.

- 2 to 3 tablespoons olive oil
- 4 cloves garlic, minced
- 1 bunch collard greens (4 to 6 leaves), stems removed, cut into 1-inch strips
- ½ teaspoon salt
- 2½ quarts water
- 1 pound pasta (orecchiette, ziti, penne, or rigatoni)

1. Heat the oil in a medium saucepan. Add the garlic and cook on low heat for about 1 minute. Add the collard greens and salt and cook on medium heat, stirring occasionally, for about 5 minutes. To steam and help soften the greens, add 2 to 3 tablespoons of water.

2. Bring the water to a boil in a medium saucepan. Add the pasta and cook for 8 or 10 minutes, or until it is tender. Drain the pasta and add it to the collard greens. Mix well and serve.

Pasta with Chard and Fennel

This is a dish of pasta and greens, seasoned with garlic, fennel, and white wine.

1 tablespoon olive oil

3 cloves garlic, minced

1 fennel bulb, trimmed and finely chopped

½ cup white wine or a nonalcoholic substitute

1 teaspoon salt

1 bunch red chard (4 to 6 leaves), stems removed (if desired) and chopped

2½ quarts water

1 pound pasta (preferably tubular)

1. Heat the oil in a medium saucepan. Add the garlic and cook on low heat for 1 minute. Add the fennel, wine, and salt and cook for about 5 minutes, or until the fennel is soft.

2. Add the chard, cover, and cook for about 5 minutes, or until the greens are tender.

3. Bring the water to a boil in a medium saucepan. Add the pasta and cook until it is just tender. Drain the pasta and add it to the chard. Cook on low heat, stirring occasionally, for about 5 minutes, or until the pasta absorbs all of the liquid.

Pasta with Leeks and Chanterelles

YIELD: 4 SERVINGS

Chanterelles are a meaty wild mushroom that grows abundantly in the woods in the fall. Make sure you get yours from a trusted source. There are similar-looking varieties that can be toxic, even lethal, but experienced mushroom hunters can easily tell the difference.

2 tablespoons olive oil

2 large leeks, cut in half lengthwise, cleaned well, and chopped

1 cup finely chopped chanterelle mushrooms

¼ cup chopped shallots

¼ cup chopped fresh parsley

6 cloves garlic, minced

1 teaspoon salt

1 cup white wine or a nonalcoholic substitute

3 tablespoons nutritional yeast flakes

2½ quarts water

1 pound pasta (preferably tubular)

1. Heat the oil in a medium saucepan. Add the leeks, mushrooms, shallots, parsley, garlic, and salt. Cook on medium-low heat, stirring occasionally, for about 5 minutes.

2. Add the wine and bring to a gentle boil. Lower the heat and let simmer for about 10 minutes. Sprinkle in the nutritional yeast and simmer for 5 minutes longer, stirring often.

3. Bring the water to a boil in a medium saucepan. Add the pasta and cook until it is just tender. Drain it well and add it to the other ingredients. Mix until well combined. Let stand for 1 to 2 minutes before serving.

Squash and Noodle Casserole

This hearty casserole is a comfort food reminiscent of classic macaroni and cheese.

1 medium acorn squash

2 tablespoons olive oil

2 leeks, cut in half lengthwise, cleaned well, and chopped

1 pound soft tofu, crumbled

3 to 4 tablespoons soy sauce

2½ quarts water

1 pound elbow macaroni

¼ cup bread crumbs

1. Cut the squash in half lengthwise and remove the seeds. Cut the halves into chunks that will fit in your vegetable steamer and steam them for 20 to 30 minutes, or until they are very soft.

2. Heat the oil in a medium saucepan. Add the leeks and cook on medium-low heat, stirring occasionally, for 5 to 10 minutes, or until they are soft.

3. When the squash is cool enough to handle, scoop the pulp into a medium bowl. Add the leeks, tofu, and soy sauce and mix well.

4. Preheat the oven to 375 degrees F and oil a 4-quart casserole dish.

5. Bring the water to a boil in a medium saucepan. Add the macaroni and cook for 6 to 8 minutes, or until it is just tender. Drain well and combine with the squash mixture.

6. Spread the mixture into the prepared casserole dish and sprinkle the bread crumbs evenly on top. Bake for 15 to 20 minutes, or until it's heated through and the bread crumbs start to brown.

Seitan Teriyaki

Seitan is a Japanese meat alternative made from the protein in wheat flour. In this recipe, it fits naturally with vegetables and classic Japanese seasonings.

3 tablespoons soy sauce

2 tablespoons rice wine or a nonalcoholic substitute

1 teaspoon unrefined cane sugar

2 cloves garlic, minced

1 pound seitan, cut into bite-size pieces

2 carrots, peeled (if desired) and chopped

2 zucchini, chopped

1 onion, sliced into rings

1 red bell pepper, sliced

1. Preheat the oven to 400 degrees F.

2. Combine the soy sauce, wine, sugar, and garlic in a small bowl. Combine the seitan, carrots, zucchini, onion, and bell pepper in a medium bowl. Add the soy sauce mixture and toss until it is evenly distributed.

3. Arrange the seitan and vegetables on a baking sheet and roast them in the oven for 20 to 30 minutes, or until they start to brown.

Bean and Squash Burgers

YIELD: 6 SERVINGS

The squash in these burgers makes a great binder. The Mexican seasonings fit naturally with the beans and squash.

1 acorn squash

1 tablespoon olive oil

½ cup diced onion

1 teaspoon salt

1 teaspoon chili powder (mild or hot)

½ teaspoon ground cumin

½ teaspoon dried oregano

2 cups cooked or canned black beans, drained

1 teaspoon red wine vinegar

1 tablespoon canola oil

Burger buns, lettuce, tomato, and the condiments of your choice

1. Cut the squash in half lengthwise and remove the seeds. Cut the halves into chunks that will fit in your vegetable steamer and steam them for 20 to 30 minutes, or until they are very soft.

2. Heat the olive oil in a small saucepan. Add the onion, salt, chili powder, cumin, and oregano. Cook on medium-low heat for about 5 minutes, or until the onion is translucent.

3. Scoop the squash pulp into a medium bowl. Stir in the onion mixture, black beans, and vinegar. Mix well.

4. Shape the mixture into 6 patties. Heat the canola oil in a medium skillet and brown the patties on both sides. Serve on buns, topped with lettuce, tomato, and condiments.

Delicata Succotash

YIELD: 6 SERVINGS

This dish celebrates the bounty of the harvest. Delicatas are an especially sweet and quick-cooking variety of winter squash. Use a good vegetable peeler or a paring knife to peel them. Wild Rice Pilaf (page 123) provides a welcome complement of flavors and textures when served with this dish.

2 tablespoons olive oil

2 medium delicata squash, peeled, cut in half, seeds removed and cut into bite-size pieces

1 leek, cut in half lengthwise, cleaned well, and chopped

4 cloves garlic, finely chopped

1 teaspoon salt

2 ripe tomatoes, cut into bite-size pieces

1 cup green beans, cut into bite-size pieces

2 cups cooked or canned white beans, drained

1 cup fresh corn kernels (2 to 3 ears)

½ cup chopped fresh basil or parsley, or a mixture of both

1. Heat the oil in a large skillet. Add the squash, leek, garlic, and salt. Cook on medium-low heat, stirring often, for about 10 minutes, or until the squash is fork-tender. Add a few tablespoons of water if the squash starts to stick.

2. Add the tomatoes and green beans. Cook on medium-high heat, stirring often, for 5 to 10 minutes, until the tomatoes start to break down and the green beans are tender.

3. Add the white beans, corn, and basil and cook until they are heated through.

Lentil Stew with Squash and Fennel

Squash and lentils thicken this hearty stew. It's a great meal for a cold, rainy day.

2 tablespoons olive oil

1 medium onion, chopped

1 cup chopped fennel bulb

3 cloves garlic, minced

1 teaspoon salt

1 delicata squash, peeled, cut in half, seeds removed, and cut into bite-size pieces

1 ripe tomato, chopped

2 cups unsalted vegetable stock or water

⅔ cup dried lentils

1 tablespoon fresh thyme, or 1 teaspoon dried

Freshly ground black pepper

1. Heat the olive oil in a medium saucepan. Add the onion, fennel, garlic, and salt. Cook for about 5 minutes on medium-low heat, or until the onion is translucent.

2. Add the squash and tomato and cook for 5 minutes.

3. Add the vegetable stock, lentils, thyme, and pepper to taste and bring the mixture to a boil. Lower the heat, cover, and cook for about 30 minutes. Remove the cover and cook for 15 minutes longer, stirring often. Taste and add additional salt, if needed.

Bell Peppers Stuffed with Black Beans

YIELD: 6 SERVINGS

These bell peppers are stuffed with beans and corn, topped with crumbled tortilla chips, and baked until they are tender enough to melt in your mouth.

1 tablespoon olive oil

1 small onion, diced

1 pasilla, poblano, or Anaheim chile, diced

1 teaspoon chili powder (mild or hot)

½ teaspoon ground cumin

½ teaspoon dried oregano

½ teaspoon salt

2 cups cooked or canned black beans, drained

1 cup fresh corn kernels (2 to 3 ears)

1 tablespoon red wine vinegar

3 medium bell peppers (any color)

2 cups Roasted Tomato Salsa (page 104)

Handful of tortilla chips

1. Preheat the oven to 375 degrees F.

2. Heat the oil in a medium saucepan. Add the onion, chile, chili powder, cumin, oregano, and salt. Cook on medium-low heat for about 5 minutes, or until the onion is translucent. Remove from the heat and stir in the black beans, corn, and vinegar.

3. Cut the bell peppers in half lengthwise and remove the seeds. Spread the salsa in the bottom of an 8-inch square baking dish. Stuff the pepper halves with the bean mixture and arrange them in the pan with the open sides facing up. Crumble the tortilla chips with your hands or crush them in a food processor until they are powdery. Sprinkle the crushed tortilla chips over the stuffed peppers.

4. Cover the pan with foil and bake the peppers in the oven for 45 to 60 minutes, or until they are very soft. Uncover them and bake for 10 minutes longer.

Black Bean Chili

This is a simple chili recipe, but it really shines with the fresh chiles and tomatoes. Use more or less of the Roasted Chile Paste, according to your taste. Serve it with rice or Masa Patties with Nuts and Vegetables (page 122).

    2 tablespoons olive oil
    1 cup chopped onion
    1 pasilla or poblano chile, finely chopped
    4 cloves garlic, minced
    1 teaspoon salt
    1 teaspoon chili powder (mild or hot)
    ½ teaspoon ground cumin
    ½ teaspoon dried oregano
    2 large tomatoes, coarsely chopped
    1 teaspoon Roasted Chile Paste (page 106)
    2 cups cooked or canned black beans, drained

1. Heat the oil in a medium saucepan. Add the onion, chile, garlic, salt, chili powder, cumin, and oregano. Cook on medium-low heat, stirring often, for about 5 minutes, or until the chile is soft and the onion is translucent.

2. Add the tomatoes and chile paste and cook on medium heat, stirring often, for 5 to 10 minutes, or until the tomatoes start to break down.

3. Add the black beans, lower the heat, and simmer for 20 minutes longer, stirring occasionally.

Cranberry Beans with Leeks and Fennel

YIELD: 4 SERVINGS

Before they are shelled, cranberry beans look like speckled green beans. Cooked, they taste like fresher, more tender versions of the dried beans we know so well. It's not difficult to remove them from the pod, and it's well worth the effort. Just split them along the seam with your fingernail and remove the beans. Some farmers sell cranberry beans already shelled. The shelled beans are pricey but so easy to use.

2 cups shelled cranberry beans (about 2 pounds unshelled)

2 tablespoons olive oil

2 leeks, sliced in half lengthwise, cleaned well, and sliced

1 fennel bulb, trimmed and cut into bite-size pieces

4 cloves garlic, minced

1 teaspoon salt

3 ripe tomatoes, coarsely chopped

½ cup chopped fresh parsley (preferably Italian)

Freshly ground black pepper

1. Place the cranberry beans in a medium saucepan, add enough water to cover, and bring to a boil. Lower the heat and cook for about 20 minutes, or until the beans are tender. Drain well.

2. While the beans are cooking, heat the oil in a skillet. Add the leeks, fennel, garlic, and salt. Cook on medium-low heat, stirring occasionally, for 5 to 10 minutes, or until the leeks and fennel are soft.

3. Add the tomatoes, parsley, and pepper to taste. Cook for 10 minutes, or until the tomatoes start to break down.

4. Add the beans to the fennel mixture. Cook for 1 to 2 minutes and serve.

Kohlrabi Slaw

YIELD: 4 SERVINGS

Kohlrabi is a bulbous vegetable in the cabbage family. Like cabbage, it makes a lovely coleslaw. If you buy it with the leaves attached, you can save the greens and cook them separately. The bulbs are sometimes green, sometimes purple. If you can find the purple ones, they will make this dish especially colorful.

¼ pound soft tofu

1 tablespoon olive oil

1 teaspoon freshly squeezed lemon juice

½ teaspoon salt

4 bulbs kohlrabi, trimmed and grated

2 medium carrots, peeled (if desired) and grated

1 tablespoon red wine vinegar

1 tablespoon finely chopped fresh dill, or 1 teaspoon dried dill weed

1. To make a creamy dressing, combine the tofu, oil, lemon juice, and salt in a food processor or blender and process until smooth.

2. Combine the kohlrabi, carrots, vinegar, and dill in a medium bowl. Add the creamy dressing and mix until evenly distributed.

Ukrainian Vegetable Salad

YIELD: 4 SERVINGS

A few years ago, I travelled to Ukraine and found that the food defied my stereotype of boiled root vegetables. This is my rendition of a salad I enjoyed on several occasions.

1 cucumber, peeled and sliced

2 dill pickles, sliced

2 carrots, peeled (if desired) and sliced

2 tablespoons chopped fresh dill

2 tablespoons chopped fresh parsley

2 tablespoons chopped fresh chives

2 tablespoons white wine vinegar

1 tablespoon olive oil

½ teaspoon salt

½ teaspoon freshly ground black pepper

Combine all of the ingredients.

Marinated Cranberry Beans

This is one of my favorite additions to a green salad, adding protein and making it into a complete meal. See page 141 for more information on cranberry beans.

1 cup shelled cranberry beans (about 1 pound unshelled)

2 tablespoons olive oil

1 tablespoon balsamic vinegar

1 tablespoon chopped fresh parsley

1 tablespoon chopped fresh chives

½ teaspoon salt

Freshly ground black pepper

1. Place the beans in a small saucepan with enough water to cover. Bring to a boil, lower the heat, and simmer for about 20 minutes, or until the beans are tender. Drain well.

2. Transfer the beans to a small bowl. Add the remaining ingredients and mix well.

Refrigerator Pickles

YIELD: 8 PICKLES

These quick pickles will keep in the refrigerator for a couple of weeks; but if you are like me, you'll finish them much faster than that.

> 1 cup water
>
> 1 cup white vinegar
>
> 1 small onion, cut in half and sliced
>
> ½ cup coarsely chopped fresh dill
>
> 6 cloves garlic, peeled
>
> 2 small hot chiles (optional)
>
> 1 teaspoon salt
>
> 8 pickling cucumbers

1. Combine the water, vinegar, onion, dill, garlic, optional chiles, and salt in a medium saucepan and bring to a boil. Cook on medium-low heat for about 10 minutes.

2. Add the whole cucumbers and cook for 5 minutes, pressing them down from time to time.

3. Remove from the heat and let cool. Store the pickles in the refrigerator, covered with the brine. They will be ready to eat in 2 to 3 hours, though they will taste even better the next day.

Mexican Vegetable Salad

This salad makes a light side dish for a Mexican meal, like Bean and Squash Burgers (page 136) or Black Bean Chili (page 140).

3 ripe tomatoes, chopped

1 cup fresh corn kernels (2 to 3 ears)

1 green bell pepper, chopped

1 zucchini, sliced into half moons

½ cup sliced black olives

1 Anaheim or poblano chile, diced

2 tablespoons red wine vinegar

1 tablespoon olive oil

1 tablespoon chili powder (mild or hot)

1 teaspoon salt

1 teaspoon ground cumin

½ teaspoon dried oregano

Combine all of the ingredients.

Mixed Vegetable Potato Salad

YIELD: 4 SERVINGS

This is a colorful potato salad with a variety of crunchy vegetables. It is most appealing when the vegetables are cut into very small pieces.

2 tablespoons olive oil

1 onion, chopped

2 cloves garlic, minced

1 cup small broccoli florets

1 cup corn kernels (2 to 3 ears)

1 carrot, peeled (if desired) and cut into thin strips

¼ cup chopped fresh parsley

1 teaspoon salt

1 quart water

4 medium potatoes (any kind but russets), unpeeled and chopped

2 tablespoons red wine vinegar

Freshly ground black pepper

1. Heat 1 tablespoon of the oil in a medium saucepan. Add the onion and garlic. Cook for about 5 minutes, or until the onion is translucent. Add the broccoli, corn, carrot, parsley, and salt. Cook for about 10 minutes, or until all of the vegetables are tender.

2. While the vegetables are cooking, bring the water to a boil in a medium saucepan. Add the potatoes and cook for about 10 minutes, until they are tender. Drain well and transfer to a bowl.

3. Add the vegetable mixture to the potatoes. Stir in the vinegar, pepper to taste, and the remaining tablespoon of oil. Chill thoroughly before serving.

Gingered Pears

YIELD: 8 SERVINGS

Serve these with vegan ice cream, or on their own for a comforting, sugar-free dessert.

    4 pears
    2 cups apple or pear juice
    2 tablespoons grated fresh ginger

1. Preheat the oven to 375 degrees F.

2. Slice the pears in half from top to bottom and remove the cores and seeds.

3. Arrange the pear halves cut side up in an 8-inch square baking dish. Combine the juice and ginger and pour the mixture over the pears.

4. Bake in the oven for about 45 minutes, or until the pears are soft. Serve warm.

Apple Strudel

YIELD: 15 SLICES

If you are lucky enough to know of a place that sells phyllo dough in the refrigerator section, rather than the freezer, you should certainly buy it there. If you buy it frozen, let it defrost in the refrigerator overnight. Don't get frustrated if some of the sheets rip or stick together. The strudel will have many layers, and when it's all rolled up together, nobody will know it's ripped except you.

> 5 apples, unpeeled and cut into small chunks
> ¼ cup apple juice
> 1 to 2 tablespoons sweetener of your choice
> 1 teaspoon vanilla extract
> 1 teaspoon white or brown rice flour
> 1 package (1 pound) phyllo dough
> 1 cup canola oil, more or less as needed

1. Combine the apples, apple juice, sweetener, and vanilla extract in a medium saucepan and cook on medium-low heat for about 5 minutes. Remove from the heat and sprinkle in the flour, stirring constantly.

2. Preheat the oven to 375 degrees F.

3. Lay a sheet of phyllo dough on a baking sheet. Using a pastry brush, coat it with some of the oil. Repeat the process with 8 sheets of the phyllo dough. Then spread one-third of the apple mixture in a line about 1 inch thick, starting about 1 inch from the bottom, and ending about 1 inch from the top. It should be 3 to 4 inches from the left side.

4. Fold the left side of the phyllo dough over the filling, fold the bottom end up 1 inch, and fold the top end down 1 inch. Roll it up from the left to the right as tightly as you can.

5. Repeat with the remaining phyllo dough and filling 2 more times, to make 3 rolls in all.

6. Score each roll by cutting into it just halfway, to make 5 pieces. Arrange the rolls on the baking sheet and brush them with another layer of the oil. Bake the rolls for about 30 minutes, or until they are golden brown. Let cool before slicing.

Chai-Spiced Mulled Cider

YIELD: ABOUT 6 CUPS

Here's a spicy variation on traditional mulled cider.

8 cups apple cider

6 cinnamon sticks

3 tablespoons chopped fresh ginger

2 tablespoons whole peppercorns

2 tablespoons whole cardamom pods

1 tablespoon whole cloves

1. Combine all of the ingredients in a large saucepan and bring to a boil.

2. Lower the heat and simmer for about 15 minutes.

3. Strain and serve.

Winter

It's hardest to find a variety of fresh foods during the winter, but it's a worthy challenge, and the results can be gratifying. During the winter months, plants store most of their nutrients underground as protection against the weather, in much the same way that we like to stay indoors where it's safe and warm. Root vegetables aren't as flamboyant as the colorful produce of summer, but they do have a depth (pardon the pun) that can be just what we need this time of year. If there is a winter farmers' market in your area, I encourage you to shop there as often as you can. It's not as exciting as it is in the summer, but the more people who go, the more exciting it becomes, as farmers will innovate in order to meet the demand. If you have no winter market, you can still select seasonal produce at the supermarket. I guarantee it will taste better than those rubbery winter tomatoes!

Winter Produce

EARLY WINTER	MID-WINTER	LATE WINTER
apples	beets	Brussels sprouts
collard greens	broccoli	celeriac
kale	rosemary	parsnips
leeks		rutabagas
mustard greens		Savoy cabbage
potatoes		turnips
winter squash		

Lentil-Barley Soup

I love this soup in part because it is so filling, and also because—except for the tomato and lemon juice—all of the ingredients are ancient Middle Eastern foods. Someone could have eaten almost the same meal six or eight thousand years ago.

2 quarts water

1 cup dried lentils

1 cup pearl barley

½ cup chopped fresh parsley

4 cloves garlic, minced

1 teaspoon salt

2 cups chopped fresh spinach (or any other greens you have available)

1 cup canned crushed tomatoes, with juice

½ cup tahini

Juice of 1 lemon

1. Bring the water to a boil. Add the lentils, barley, parsley, garlic, and salt. Cook on medium-low heat for 20 to 30 minutes, stirring occasionally.

2. Stir in the spinach, tomatoes, and tahini. Cook for 10 minutes, or until the lentils and barley are very tender. Stir in the lemon juice and serve.

Cabbage-Potato Soup

YIELD: 6 SERVINGS

The mustard and caraway in this recipe bring me back to my childhood, eating deli food in Brooklyn.

    6 cups unsalted vegetable stock or water

    1 small head cabbage, shredded

    4 medium potatoes (any kind but russets), unpeeled and cubed

    1 large onion, diced

    4 cloves garlic, minced

    2 teaspoons dried dill weed

    1 teaspoon salt

    1 teaspoon whole caraway seeds

    2 tablespoons prepared yellow mustard

1. Combine the stock, cabbage, potatoes, onion, garlic, dill weed, salt, and caraway seeds in a medium soup pot and bring to a boil. Cook on medium-low heat, stirring occasionally, for 30 to 40 minutes, or until the potatoes start to break down.

2. Stir in the mustard. Taste and add additional salt, if needed. Cook for 5 minutes longer and serve.

Portuguese Kale and White Bean Soup

Not much grows in Portugal, but this soup shows off what does grow there.

4 cups unsalted vegetable stock or water

1 bunch curly leaf kale (6 to 8 leaves), finely shredded

½ cup white wine or a nonalcoholic substitute

8 cloves garlic, minced

1 tablespoon nutritional yeast flakes

1 teaspoon salt

2 cups cooked or canned white beans, drained

Freshly ground black pepper

1. Combine the stock, kale, wine, garlic, nutritional yeast, and salt in a medium soup pot. Bring to a boil, lower the heat, and cook for 20 to 30 minutes.

2. Stir in the beans and pepper to taste and cook for 5 to 10 minutes longer.

Vegetable-Barley Soup

YIELD: 4 SERVINGS

This hearty soup takes almost no attention. Just toss everything in the pot and cook it until it's done.

6 cups unsalted vegetable stock

½ cup pearl barley

1 carrot, peeled (if desired) and finely chopped

1 parsnip, peeled and finely chopped

1 stalk celery, finely chopped

1 medium red or Yukon Gold potato, unpeeled and finely chopped

½ cup chopped fresh parsley

1 shallot, minced

4 cloves garlic, minced

1 teaspoon dried dill weed

1 teaspoon salt

½ teaspoon freshly ground black pepper

Combine all of the ingredients in a medium soup pot. Bring to a boil, lower the heat, and cook for about 30 minutes, or until the barley is soft.

YIELD: 6 SERVINGS

Curried Vegetable Soup

This soup has a variety of colorful vegetables in a thick, curried legume base.

6 cups unsalted vegetable stock or water

2 cups dried red lentils or yellow split peas

1 onion, chopped

1 tablespoon peeled and grated fresh ginger

1 tablespoon ground cumin

2 cloves garlic, minced

1 teaspoon salt

1 teaspoon ground turmeric

½ teaspoon ground cardamom

½ teaspoon ground coriander

2 carrots, peeled (if desired) and chopped

2 medium potatoes (any kind except russets), chopped

1 cup chopped cauliflower

1 cup broccoli florets

Cayenne

1 small can (6 ounces) coconut milk

1. Bring the stock to a boil in a medium soup pot. Add the lentils, onion, ginger, cumin, garlic, salt, turmeric, cardamom, and coriander and cook on medium-low heat for 10 to 15 minutes. Add the carrots and potatoes and cook for about 15 minutes, stirring often.

2. Add the cauliflower, broccoli, and cayenne to taste and cook for 15 to 20 minutes, or until all of the vegetables and the lentils are soft. Stir in the coconut milk, cook for 1 minute longer, and serve.

Gold Beets with Leeks and Chives

YIELD: 4 SERVINGS

Gold beets taste a lot like the red ones, but they don't bleed into every-thing around them. Substitute red beets if you can't find gold ones. If you can't find fresh chives, fresh parsley also works well.

1 pound gold beets, trimmed

2 tablespoons olive oil

1 medium leek, cut in half lengthwise, cleaned well, and chopped

2 to 3 cloves garlic, minced

½ teaspoon salt

Freshly ground black pepper

¼ cup chopped fresh chives

2 tablespoons balsamic vinegar

1. Place the beets in a medium saucepan, add enough water to cover, and bring to a boil. Cook on medium heat for 45 to 60 minutes, or until the skins can be rubbed off with your fingers. (To test one, fish it out of the pot with a pair of tongs and run it under cold water until it's cool enough to handle.)

2. While the beets are cooking, heat the oil in a small saucepan. Add the leek, garlic, salt, and pepper to taste. Cook on medium-low heat for about 5 minutes, or until the leek is soft. Remove from the heat and stir in the chives and vinegar.

3. Peel the beets using your fingers and cut them into bite-size pieces. Add the beets to the leek mixture and toss until well combined. Serve hot or at room temperature.

Pickled Beets

This colorful side dish is high in iron and rich in flavor.

6 medium beets, trimmed

1 tablespoon olive oil

1 small onion, diced

2 tablespoons chopped fresh dill, or 1 teaspoon dried dill weed

½ teaspoon salt

Freshly ground black pepper

¼ cup water

2 to 3 tablespoons white vinegar

1. Place the beets in a medium saucepan, add enough water to cover, and bring to a boil. Cook on medium heat for 45 to 60 minutes, or until the skins can be rubbed off with your fingers. (To test one, fish it out of the pot with a pair of tongs and run it under cold water until it's cool enough to handle.)

2. While the beets are cooking, heat the olive oil in a small saucepan. Add the onion, dill, salt, and pepper to taste and cook for about 5 minutes, or until the onion is translucent. Add the water and vinegar, bring to a boil, lower the heat, and simmer for 5 minutes longer.

3. Peel the beets using your fingers and cut them into bite-size pieces. Toss the beets with the onion mixture. Cool before serving. Stored in the refrigerator, the beets will keep for at least 1 week.

Broccoli Romana

You can serve this tasty broccoli dish as a side, or add a cup of cooked chickpeas or white beans and turn it into a main course.

3 cups broccoli florets (or a combination of florets and peeled and chopped stems)

1 to 2 tablespoons olive oil

1 leek, cut in half lengthwise, cleaned well, and chopped

3 shallots, diced

3 cloves garlic, minced

1 teaspoon dried basil

½ teaspoon dried oregano

½ teaspoon salt

Freshly ground black pepper

1. Steam the broccoli florets for 1 to 2 minutes.

2. Heat the olive oil in a medium saucepan. Add the leek, shallots, garlic, basil, oregano, salt, and pepper to taste. Cook on medium-low heat for about 5 minutes, or until the leek is soft and the shallots are translucent.

3. Add the steamed broccoli and cook for 1 minute longer.

Braised Turnips

Turnips lend themselves well to braising. Like other root vegetables, they are appealing when cooked until soft, and they hold flavors well.

⅓ cup Marsala wine or unsalted vegetable stock

⅓ cup water

¼ cup chopped fresh parsley

2 to 3 tablespoons chopped fresh chives

4 cloves garlic, minced

½ teaspoon salt

½ teaspoon freshly ground black pepper

1 pound turnips, trimmed and chopped

1. Combine the wine, water, parsley, chives, garlic, salt, and pepper in a medium saucepan and bring to a boil. Add the turnips.

2. Cover and cook on medium-low heat for about 20 minutes, or until the turnips are soft.

Leek and Parsnip Sauté

YIELD: 4 SERVINGS

I love the full, sweet flavor of parsnips. Choose small ones, as they are less likely to be woody in the center.

> 1 tablespoon olive oil
>
> 2 leeks, cut in half lengthwise, cleaned well, and chopped
>
> 2 cloves garlic, minced
>
> 3 parsnips, peeled and chopped
>
> 3 tablespoons chopped fresh parsley
>
> ½ teaspoon salt
>
> ½ cup pitted kalamata or black olives, sliced

1. Heat the olive oil in a medium saucepan. Add the leeks and garlic and cook on medium-low heat for about 5 minutes.

2. Add the parsnips, parsley, and salt and cook, stirring occasionally, for 5 to 10 minutes, or until the parsnips are soft.

3. Stir in the olives and cook for 2 to 3 minutes longer.

Savoy Cabbage with Cashews

Savoy cabbage has curly leaves and a delicate flavor. Make sure to remove the outer leaves, as they can be tough.

1 tablespoon olive oil

1 leek, cut in half lengthwise, cleaned well, and chopped

3 cloves garlic, minced

½ teaspoon salt

Freshly ground black pepper

1 medium Savoy cabbage, cored and chopped

½ cup roasted cashews

2 to 3 tablespoons Marsala wine or unsalted vegetable stock

1. Heat the oil in a medium saucepan. Add the leek, garlic, salt, and pepper to taste. Cook on medium-low heat for about 5 minutes, or until the leek is tender.

2. Add the cabbage, cashews, and wine. Cover and cook for about 10 minutes, or until the cabbage is soft.

Roasted Brussels Sprouts with Lemon-Garlic Sauce

YIELD: 4 SERVINGS

Like okra, Brussels sprouts have a terrible reputation. Don't dismiss them until you try this recipe. It's a winter favorite in my household.

1 pound Brussels sprouts, trimmed and quartered lengthwise
¼ cup olive oil
¾ teaspoon salt
¼ teaspoon freshly ground black pepper
6 cloves garlic, unpeeled
1 teaspoon freshly squeezed lemon juice

1. Preheat the oven to 400 degrees F.

2. Toss the Brussels sprouts with 2 tablespoons of the oil, ½ teaspoon of the salt, and all of the pepper. Arrange them on a baking sheet.

3. Toss the garlic cloves with enough of the oil to coat them, wrap them in foil, and place them in a separate corner of the same baking sheet.

4. Roast the Brussels sprouts and the garlic in the oven for about 30 minutes, or until the Brussels sprouts start to brown and the garlic becomes aromatic.

5. When the garlic is cool enough to handle, squeeze the pulp out of the skins into a small bowl and mash it with a fork. Mix the garlic pulp with the remaining oil, the remaining ¼ teaspoon of salt, and all of the lemon juice to make a sauce. Serve the sauce on the side as a dip. Alternatively, toss the roasted Brussels sprouts with the sauce before serving.

Glazed Root Vegetables

YIELD: 4 SERVINGS

In this recipe, the vegetables are first braised until they are tender, then they are finished by cooking off the liquid to give them a sweet, thick coating. Chioggia beets are white inside, with pink concentric circles. Like yellow beets, they have a flavor similar to the red ones, but they don't bleed into everything around them.

¼ cup balsamic vinegar

2 tablespoons olive oil

1 tablespoon chopped fresh rosemary

½ teaspoon salt

Freshly ground black pepper

1 cup peeled and chopped carrots

1 cup peeled and chopped parsnips

1 cup chopped turnips

1 cup peeled and chopped Chioggia or yellow beets

1. Combine the vinegar, oil, rosemary, salt, and pepper to taste in a medium saucepan and bring to a boil.

2. Add the carrots, parsnips, turnips, and beets and return to a boil. Lower the heat, cover, and simmer for about 20 minutes, or until the vegetables are just tender. You can cook them a little longer if you like them very soft.

3. Remove the cover, turn up the heat, and cook, stirring constantly, for a few minutes, or until all of the liquid evaporates and the vegetables have a thick, syrupy coating.

Roasted Root Vegetables

Your home will fill with a heavenly aroma as you roast these winter vegetables. You can add any other root vegetables you like.

- 1 medium potato (any kind but russet), chopped
- 2 turnips, trimmed and chopped
- 1 carrot, peeled (if desired) and chopped
- 1 parsnip, peeled and chopped
- 1 leek, cut in half lengthwise, cleaned well, and chopped
- ¼ cup chopped fresh parsley
- 2 to 3 tablespoons olive oil
- 2 tablespoons finely chopped fresh rosemary
- 1 teaspoon salt
- Freshly ground black pepper

1. Preheat the oven to 400 degrees F.
2. Place the potato in a small saucepan with enough water to cover. Bring to a boil, lower the heat, and cook for 1 to 2 minutes. Drain well.
3. Transfer the potato to a bowl, add the remaining ingredients, and toss until evenly combined.
4. Arrange the vegetables on a baking sheet and roast them in the oven for 30 to 40 minutes, or until they start to brown.

Squash and Greens

You can use any squash you have on hand for this recipe. Butternut and kabocha are the easiest to peel. You can use a different variety of greens as well, but if you use something tough like collards or kale, allow more cooking time and use extra liquid.

2 to 3 tablespoons olive oil

1 pound winter squash, peeled and cut into 1-inch cubes

¼ cup chopped leek or shallots

¼ cup red wine or unsalted vegetable stock

2 tablespoons chopped fresh rosemary

3 to 4 cloves garlic, minced

½ teaspoon salt

2 cups fresh spinach, cleaned and chopped

1 to 2 tablespoons balsamic vinegar

1. Heat the oil in a medium saucepan. Add the squash, leek, wine, rosemary, garlic, and salt. Cook on medium-low heat, stirring often, for 10 to 15 minutes, or until the squash is soft.

2. Add the spinach and cook for 3 to 4 minutes, or until it wilts. Remove from the heat and stir in the balsamic vinegar.

Seitan Shepherd's Pie

When you chop seitan in a food processor, it acquires a texture similar to ground beef that works well in this winter comfort food.

1 pound white potatoes, peeled (if desired) and quartered

½ cup unsweetened soymilk

1 teaspoon salt

1 tablespoon olive oil

1 onion, chopped

2 cloves garlic, minced

1 teaspoon dried basil

½ teaspoon dried marjoram

½ teaspoon dried thyme

1 pound seitan

½ cup canned crushed tomatoes, with juice

1. Place the potatoes in a medium saucepan and add enough water to cover them. Bring to a boil, lower the heat, and simmer for 10 to 15 minutes, or until the potatoes are soft. Drain them well, transfer to a bowl, and mash them. Stir in the soymilk and ½ teaspoon of the salt.

2. While the potatoes are cooking, heat the oil in a medium saucepan. Add the onion, garlic, the remaining ½ teaspoon of salt, and all of the basil, marjoram, and thyme. Cook for about 5 minutes, or until the onion is translucent.

3. Chop the seitan in a food processor using the pulse button for about 10 seconds, until it's the consistency of ground beef. Add the seitan and tomatoes to the onion mixture.

4. Preheat the oven to 375 degrees F.

5. Spread the seitan mixture on the bottom of an 8-inch square casserole dish and top it with the mashed potatoes. Bake for about 15 minutes, until heated through.

Tofu Scramble

YIELD: 4 SERVINGS

This medley makes a great breakfast item.

2 medium potatoes (any kind but russets), cut into bite-size pieces

2 tablespoons olive oil

1 leek, cut in half lengthwise, cleaned well, and chopped

4 cloves garlic, minced

½ teaspoon salt

2 cups chopped greens (kale, collard greens, spinach, or mustard greens)

1 pound soft tofu

1 tablespoon nutritional yeast flakes

1 tablespoon vegan Worcestershire sauce

1. Cook the potatoes in boiling water to cover for 2 to 3 minutes. Drain well and set aside.

2. Heat the oil in a medium saucepan. Add the leek, garlic, and salt. Cook on medium-low heat for 2 to 3 minutes. Add the greens and cook, stirring often, for about 10 minutes, or until they are tender. If you are using kale or collard greens, sprinkle in a few tablespoons of water to help soften them.

3. Add the potatoes and cook for a few minutes longer, until they are tender.

4. Mash the tofu with a fork. Add it to the vegetable mixture along with the nutritional yeast and Worcestershire sauce. Cook for 3 to 4 minutes, until it is heated through.

Mixed Greens with Seitan

This is one of my favorite meals. I prefer the greens cooked until they are just tender, but if you like them very soft, you can cook them longer.

2 tablespoons olive oil

1 onion, diced

4 cloves garlic, minced

½ teaspoon salt

2 bunches kale, mustard greens, or collard greens (4 to 6 leaves per bunch), trimmed and sliced, or 1/2 pound braising mix

½ pound seitan, cut into bite-size pieces

2 tablespoons vegan Worcestershire sauce

1. Heat the olive oil in a medium skillet. Add the onion, garlic, and salt. Cook on medium-low heat for about 5 minutes, or until the onion is translucent.

2. Add the greens a handful at a time, adding more when they cook down. Sprinkle in 2 to 3 tablespoons of water if the mixture seems too dry. Cook for 5 to 10 minutes, or until the greens are tender.

3. Add the seitan and Worcestershire sauce and cook for 5 minutes, until it is heated through.

Winter Stuffed Cabbage

This stuffed cabbage is topped with a hearty mushroom gravy.

1½ cups water

¾ cup brown rice

2 tablespoons olive oil

½ cup chopped onion

1 teaspoon dried basil

½ teaspoon dried thyme

½ teaspoon salt

6 to 8 button mushrooms, sliced

1 tablespoon white or brown rice flour

½ cup water

1 tablespoon soy sauce

1 medium head cabbage

1. Bring the water to a boil in a small saucepan. Stir in the rice, return to a boil, lower the heat, cover, and cook for 30 to 40 minutes, until all of the liquid is absorbed.

2. Heat the oil in a medium saucepan. Add the onion, basil, thyme, and salt. Cook for about 5 minutes, or until the onion is translucent. Add the mushrooms and cook for 3 to 4 minutes, until they start to release their liquid. Stir in the flour and mix well. Then stir in the water and soy sauce. Bring the mixture slowly to a boil. Lower the heat and cook, stirring constantly, for 1 to 2 minutes, or until the mixture thickens into a sauce.

3. When the rice is ready, mix half of the mushroom sauce with it and set the rest of the sauce aside.

4. Preheat the oven to 375 degrees F.

5. Bring 2 to 3 quarts of water to a boil in a large stockpot. Immerse the head of cabbage, holding it under the water with a pair of tongs. After about 2 minutes, remove and drain it. When it is cool enough to handle, gently peel off the outer leaves. If you don't get 8 intact

leaves about the size of your hand, submerge the head again and peel off a few more leaves as they soften.

6. Trim the stiff part from the bottom of each leaf. Place a few table-spoons of the rice mixture in the center of 1 leaf. Roll it up from the bottom, folding the sides over and in as you continue rolling. Repeat with the remaining leaves and the remaining rice mixture.

7. Place the rolls in an 8-inch square baking dish with the seams fac-ing down and cover them with the remaining mushroom sauce. Cover the pan with foil and bake in the oven for about 30 minutes, or until the cabbage is very soft.

Beet and Walnut Salad

YIELD: 4 SERVINGS

The rich, deep color of beets make them a wonderful base for a salad. In this recipe, they are served with walnuts and a lemon vinaigrette dressing.

4 medium beets, trimmed

½ cup chopped walnuts

4 green onions, sliced

¼ cup chopped fresh parsley

Juice of 1 lemon

2 tablespoons olive oil

½ teaspoon salt

1. Place the beets in a medium saucepan, add enough water to cover, and bring to a boil. Cook on medium heat for 45 to 60 minutes, or until the skins can be rubbed off with your fingers. (To test one, fish it out of the pot with a pair of tongs and run it under cold water until it's cool enough to handle.)

2. Peel the beets using your fingers and cut them into bite-size pieces. Add the remaining ingredients and mix well.

Apple Crisp

Serve this crisp warm, right out of the oven. You can prepare both the filling and topping ahead of time, but keep them separate until you are ready to assemble the dessert and pop it in the oven.

TOPPING

¾ cup nonhydrogenated margarine, softened

¾ cup unrefined cane sugar

1¾ cups unbleached white or whole wheat flour

1 teaspoon salt

½ teaspoon baking soda

1 cup rolled oats

FILLING

½ cup apple juice

6 apples (any variety), unpeeled, cored, and cut into bite-size pieces

1 to 2 tablespoons sweetener of your choice (optional)

½ teaspoon ground cinnamon

1 to 2 tablespoons white or brown rice flour

1. Preheat the oven to 375 degrees F.

2. To make the topping, combine the margarine and sugar in a medium bowl. Combine the wheat flour, salt, and baking soda in a separate bowl. Stir the flour mixture into the margarine mixture and mix until fairly smooth. Add the oats and mix well. The mixture will be crumbly, but it should hold together when squeezed.

3. To make the filling, heat the juice in a medium saucepan. Add the apples, optional sweetener, and cinnamon. Cook on medium-low heat, stirring often, for about 10 minutes, or until the apples start to break down. Sprinkle in the rice flour, stirring constantly.

4. Pour the filling into an 8-inch square baking dish and crumble the topping mixture evenly over it. Bake for 25 to 30 minutes, or until the topping starts to brown.

Glossary

BARLEY. One of the oldest cultivated grains, barley has been a traditional food in Europe and the Middle East for millennia. It has recently enjoyed an upsurge in popularity as the natural food movement has grown. It is often sold in bulk, by the pound. Pearl barley is the kind most commonly found and used. It has had the bran and inedible outer husk removed and has been steamed and polished.

CAPERS. Capers are the pickled buds of a shrub that grows in Mediterranean regions. They are about half the size of peas and are usually sold in small jars. They have lots of flavor and nicely complement olives, but they should be used sparingly because they can overpower other ingredients.

COCONUT MILK. A sweet, creamy product made from the meat of coconuts, coconut milk is often used in tropical and Asian cuisines. It is high in saturated fat, but there is some disagreement among nutritionists over whether it is actually unhealthful. Coconut milk is extremely tasty, and I like to use it in moderation. It is usually sold in cans, and some grocery stores also offer low-fat varieties. I use the full-fat kind, with restraint.

CORN GRITS. Made from coarsely ground cornmeal, corn grits are mixed with boiling water, olive oil, and salt to make Italian polenta, a thick porridge that when cooled can be sliced or served in chunks. In Southern cooking, corn grits are often served as a breakfast food.

ISRAELI COUSCOUS. Also known as "Middle Eastern couscous," Israeli couscous is a toasted pasta shaped like small balls. It has a great mouthfeel and works especially well in salads. You can find it in Middle Eastern grocery stores and specialty food stores.

MARSALA WINE. A sweet white dessert wine, Marsala is often used in Italian cuisine. It should be added to dishes at least five minutes before they are done, so the alcohol can cook off. If you would prefer a nonalcoholic alternative, use unsalted vegetable stock instead.

MASA HARINA. Masa harina is a flour made from ground corn that has been mixed with limewater (water plus calcium oxide). The process of adding something alkaline to corn boosts nutrients as well as flavor. In parts of the United States where there are large Hispanic populations, you can often buy masa harina in five-pound bags in grocery stores.

NORI. Nori is a sea vegetable that comes in pressed sheets; it is commonly used for sushi. You can buy nori in Asian grocery stores and natural food stores, although the packages in Asian stores tend to be dramatically less expensive. Nori is usually toasted before being used, which gives it a greenish tint. You can buy it already toasted, or you can toast it yourself by holding it about a foot from a flame or electric burner for a few seconds, until it changes color.

NUTRITIONAL YEAST FLAKES. Sometimes called "brewer's yeast" (although the two yeasts are not the same), nutritional yeast is used as both a natural flavor enhancer and nutritional supplement. It is high in B vitamins and has a nutty taste, which can add depth to other flavors in a dish.

ORZO. A variety of pasta shaped like rice, orzo is commonly used in Greek cuisine. Cook orzo in boiling water, like other pasta. It cooks quickly and should be stirred almost constantly, because it tends to stick together and cling to the bottom of the pot.

PINE NUTS. Rich, oily seeds from pine trees, pine nuts are often used in Italian dishes, especially pesto. They tend to be quite expensive, but they are exceptional and worth using, if only on special occasions.

QUINOA. A high-protein grain indigenous to Peru, quinoa mostly grows at high altitudes. Some experts say that quinoa must be rinsed before it is cooked or else it gets slimy or has a bitter taste, but I haven't found this to be the case.

SEITAN. A high-protein meat alternative made from vital wheat gluten, or instant gluten flour, seitan is chewy and absorbs flavor well. There are quite a few brands of commercially available seitan, but it's not difficult to make it yourself. I provide a recipe for making it from scratch in my first cookbook, *The Accidental Vegan*.

TAHINI. A sesame paste commonly used in Middle Eastern foods, tahini has a consistency similar to runny peanut butter. There are domestically produced organic brands available, but they are often very thick and don't taste quite authentic. I personally prefer the brands that are made by companies who specialize in Middle Eastern foods.

TOFU. Also known as "bean curd," tofu is a high-protein food made from soybeans. It comes in white cakes with varying degrees of firmness. Use firm or extra-firm tofu in recipes where you want it to hold together as chunks, and use soft tofu in dishes where you are crumbling or puréeing it. Tofu is usually sold refrigerated and covered in water, which keeps it fresh. Store leftover tofu in fresh water in the refrigerator, and change the water every day or two.

VEGAN WORCESTERSHIRE SAUCE. Worcestershire sauce is a tasty condiment based on an all-purpose sauce that was developed in England from an Indian recipe during the nineteenth century. The traditional version contains anchovies; the vegan version does not. There are several commercially available brands of vegan Worcestershire sauce, and there's a recipe for it in my first cookbook, *The Accidental Vegan*.

Index

Recipe titles appear it *italic* typeface.

A

acorn squash, 14
  in *Squash and Noodle Casserole,* 134
  in *Squash Burgers, Bean and,* 136
  in *Squash Soup, Harvest Corn and,* 111
  in *Squash with Roasted Garlic, Velvety,* 120
  and Wild Rice Patties, 126
Afghani Spinach, 40
Afghan seasoning combinations, 24
agriculture, 3
almond(s)
  Cake, Raspberry-, 97
  Haricots Verts with Slivered, 63
  in *Nuts and Vegetables, Masa Patties with,* 122
Anaheim chiles, 9
animal fats, 21
Anselmo's Organic Farm, 1
appetizers
  Baby Artichokes with Basil "Mayonnaise," Panfried, 68
  Baby Pattypans, Stuffed, 71
  Cipollini Onions, Balsamic, 73
  Eggplant, Stuffed, 78
  Green Bean-Walnut Pâté, 57
  Salsa, Peach, 58
  salsa, *Pico de Gallo,* 106
  Salsa, Roasted Tomatillo, 105
  Salsa, Roasted Tomato, 104

  Squash, Parsnip, and Fennel Bruschetta, 107
  Squash Hummus, 102
  Tomatoes, Pesto Stuffed, 65
  Veggie-Walnut Pinwheels, 108–9
Apple Crisp, 172
Apple Strudel, 149
Apricots with Hazelnuts, Caramelized, 99
Armenian Stewed Eggplant, 81
Artichokes with Basil "Mayonnaise," Panfried Baby, 68
Arugula and Cherry Tomatoes, Pasta with Wilted, 82
Arugula Pesto, Fennel and, 56
Asian cabbages, 7
Asian condiment, *Roasted Chile Paste,* 106
asparagus
  breaking, 34
  Curry, Leek and, 43
  with Ginger Sauce, 35
  with Mustard-Dill Sauce, 34
  in *Polenta Primavera,* 44
  and Potato Soup, Puréed, 30

B

baby dishes/produce
  Artichokes with Basil "Mayonnaise," Panfried, 68
  Bok Choy with Tofu, 45
  Carrots with Fresh Thyme, Roasted, 33
  Pattypans, Stuffed, 71

potatoes, 14
Ballard Farmers' Market, 1, 2
Balsamic Cipollini Onions, 73
barbecuing (grilling), 20–21
barley, 173
  Salad with Fresh Fava Beans, Lentil-, 89
  Soup, Lentil-, 152
  Soup, Vegetable-, 155
Bars, Blueberry, 95
basil, 11
  "Mayonnaise," Panfried Baby Artichokes with, 68
  in *Pesto, Sicilian,* 55
  Summer Squash with, 73
bean curd (tofu). *See* tofu (bean curd)
bean(s). *See also* specific types of
  Dilly, 75
  with Garlic Scapes, White, 41
  Pickled Sea, 38
  Salad, Three, 94
  and Squash Burgers, 136
beefsteak tomatoes, 16
beet(s)
  Greens with Young Garlic, 32
  with Leeks and Chives, Gold, 157
  Pickled, 158
  roasting, 21
  in *Vegetables, Glazed Root,* 164
  and Walnut Salad, 171
bell pepper(s)
  -Stuffed with Black Beans, 139
  grilling/roasting, 20

in *Lentils with Fennel and Sweet Peppers*, 83
in *Pepperonata*, 103
in *Peppers, White Beans with Roasted*, 85
in *Polenta Primavera*, 44
in *Salad, Israeli*, 91
in *Vegetable Medley, Summer*, 76
in *Vegetables, Mexican Roasted*, 127
Berry Compote, Mixed, 98
beverage, *Chai-Spiced Mulled Cider*, 150
black bean(s)
   in *Bean and Squash Burgers*, 136
   Chile, 140
   Simple, 130
   Bell Peppers Stuffed with, 139
black pepper, 8–9
blending flavors, 23
blueberry(ies)
   Bars, 95
   Cobbler, Nectarine and, 100
   in *Mixed Berry Compote*, 98
boiling, 22
bok choy, 7
Bok Choy with Tofu, Baby, 45
braising/braised dishes, 19
   Carrots with Cranberries, 121
   Turnips, 160
Brazilian Collard Greens, 118
bread, in *Pumpkin Seed Stuffing*, 125
bread, sauce for, *Roasted Garlic and Herb*, 27
breakfast dishes
   corn grits, 173
   Peach-Pecan Cake, 96
   Tofu Scramble, 168
brewer's yeast (nutritional yeast flakes), 174
broccoli
   Romana, 159
   in *Vegetable Potato Salad, Mixed*, 147
   in *Vegetable Salad, Solstice Steamed*, 47
   in *Vegetable Soup, Curried*, 156

in *Vegetable Soup with Orzo, Greek*, 113
in *Veggie-Walnut Pinwheels*, 108–9
Bruschetta, Squash, Parsnip, and Fennel, 107
bruschetta sauce, *Caponata*, 54
bruschetta sauce, *Pesto, Fennel and Arugula*, 56
brussels sprouts, 7–8
Brussels Sprouts with Lemon-Garlic Sauce, Roasted, 163
Burgers, Bean and Squash, 136
butterball potatoes, 14
butternut squash, 14
   in *Soup, Couscous and Roasted Pepper*, 114
   in *Squash and Greens*, 166
button mushrooms, in *Stuffed Cabbage, Winter*, 170–71
button mushrooms, in *Vegetables, Mexican Roasted*, 127

C

cabbage(s), 7–8. *See also* specific types of
   braising, 19
   in *Coleslaw, Picnic*, 92
   cooking, 7–8
   grilling, advice against, 21
   -Potato Soup, 153
   Summer Stuffed, 80–81
   Winter Stuffed, 170–71
Cajun seasoning combinations, 24
Cake, Peach-Pecan, 96
Cake, Raspberry-Almond, 97
California chiles, 10
capers, 173
Caramelized Apricots with Hazelnuts, 99
caraway, in *Cabbage-Potato Soup*, 153
cardamom, in *Chai-Spiced Mulled Cider*, 150
Caribbean Pumpkin-Coconut Soup, 112
carrot(s)

with *Cranberries, Braised*, 121
with *Fresh Thyme, Roasted Baby*, 33
and *Jalapeño Chiles, Pickled*, 129
in *Picnic Coleslaw*, 92
in *Roasted Root Vegetables*, 165
roasting, 21
in *Salad, Mixed Vegetable Potato*, 147
in *Salad, Solstice Steamed Vegetable*, 47
in *Salad, Ukrainian Vegetable*, 143
sautéing, 21
in *Seitan Teriyaki*, 135
in *Slaw, Kohlrabi*, 142
Soup, Roasted Leek and, 28
in *Soup, Curried Vegetable*, 156
in *Soup, Vegetable-Barley*, 155
in *Soup with Orzo, Greek Vegetable*, 113
in *Vegetables, Glazed Root*, 164
in *Vegetables, Greek Stewed*, 74
in *Vegetables, Mexican Roasted*, 127
Cashews, Savoy Cabbage with, 162
Casserole, Squash and Noodle, 134
casserole, winter squash in, 15–16
cauliflower, in *Soup, Curried Vegetable*, 156
cauliflower, in *Veggie-Walnut Pinwheels*, 108–9
celery, in *Soup, Vegetable-Barley*, 155
celery, in *Soup with Orzo, Greek Vegetable*, 113
Chai-Spiced Mulled Cider, 150
Chanterelles, Pasta with Leeks and, 133
Chanterelles in Wine Sauce, Wine and, 119
chard, 10, 11
   and *Chanterelles in Wine Sauce*, 119
   and *Fennel, Pasta with*, 132
   in *Greens, Greek*, 117

in *Polenta Primavera*, 44
sautéing, 21–22
in *Vegetable Salad, Solstice Steamed*, 47
cherry tomatoes, 16
   Orzo with Fennel and Roasted, 86
   Pasta with Wilted Arugula and, 82
   Purslane with Shaved Fennel and, 93
   in *Salad, Roasted Eggplant Pasta*, 87
   in *Vegetable Medley, Summer*, 76
Chez Panisse, 5
chickpea(s)
   in *Curry, Leek and Asparagus*, 43
   Green Beans with, 77
   in *Minestrone*, 60
   Salad, Middle Eastern, 88
chile(s), 8–10. *See also* specific types of
   in *Bell Peppers Stuffed with Black Beans*, 139
   in *Chili, Black Bean*, 140
   cooking with/roasting, 9
   dried, 9–10
   handling, 9
   Paste, Roasted, 106
   in *Patties with Nuts and Vegetables, Masa*, 122
   in *Pickles, Refrigerator*, 145
   in *Salad, Mexican Vegetable*, 146
   in salsas, 9, 10, 58, 104, 105, 106
   in *Soup, Caribbean Pumpkin-Coconut*, 112
   in *Soup, Harvest Corn and Squash*, 111
   Squash Blossoms with, 61
Chili, Black Bean, 140
Chinese chiles, 9–10
Chinese dish, *Asparagus with Ginger Sauce*, 35
Chinese dish, *Baby Bok Choy with Tofu*, 45
Chinese seasoning combinations, 24

Chioggia beets, in *Glazed Root Vegetables*, 164
chives, 12–13
Chives, Gold Beets with Leeks and, 157
Chocolate-Dipped Strawberries, 50
Cider, Chai-Spiced Mulled, 150
cilantro, 11
Cilantro-Lime Dressing, 102
Cipollini Onions, Balsamic, 73
cloves, in *Chai-Spiced Mulled Cider*, 150
Cobbler, Nectarine and Blueberry, 100
coconut milk, 173
Coconut Soup, Caribbean Pumpkin-, 112
coleslaw, 8
   Kohlrabi, 142
   Picnic, 92
collard greens, 10
   braising, 19
   Brazilian, 118
   in *Greens, Greek*, 117
   in *Greens, Squash and*, 166
   in *Greens with Seitan, Mixed*, 169
   Pasta with, 131
   sautéing, 21
   in *Scramble, Tofu*, 168
   in *Soup, Caribbean Pumpkin-Coconut*, 112
   in *Soup, West African Peanut*, 29
Community Supported Agriculture (CSA), 51
condiment, *Pico de Gallo*, 106
condiment, *Roasted Chile Paste*, 106
convenience foods, 6
cooking simply, 5–6
corn
   in *Bell Peppers Stuffed with Black Beans*, 139
   on the Cob, Herb-Roasted, 70
   and Squash Soup, Harvest, 111
   in *Succotash, Delicata*, 137
   in *Vegetable Medley, Summer*, 76
   in *Vegetable Potato Salad, Mixed*, 147

   in *Vegetable Salad, Mexican*, 146
corn grits, 173
Couscous and Roasted Pepper Soup, 114
Couscous with Fresh Fava Beans, Israeli, 90
Cranberries, Braised Carrots with, 121
Cranberries, Wild Rice with, 124
Cranberry Beans, Marinated, 144
Cranberry Beans with Leeks and Fennel, 141
Crisp, Apple, 172
CSA (Community Supported Agriculture), 51
cucumber(s)
   Pickles, Refrigerator, 145
   Salad, Curried, 93
   in *Salad, Israeli*, 91
   in *Salad, Ukrainian Vegetable*, 143
   Sushi Roll (Kappa Maki), 72
cuisine flavor listing, 24
curly leaf kale, 10
curry(ied)
   Cucumber Salad, 93
   Leek and Asparagus, 43
   Vegetable Soup, 156

D

delicata squash, 14, 15
   in *Squash, Parsnip and Fennel Bruschetta*, 107
   in *Squash and Fennel, Lentil Stew with*, 138
   Succotash, 137
desserts
   Apple Crisp, 172
   Apple Strudel, 149
   Apricots with Hazelnuts, Caramelized, 99
   Berry Compote, Mixed, 98
   Blueberry Bars, 95
   Nectarine and Blueberry Cobbler, 100
   Peach Pecan Cake, 96
   Pears, Gingered, 148

Raspberry-Almond Cake, 97
Strawberries, Chocolate-Dipped, 50
Strawberry-Rhubarb Tart, 49
dill(y), 12
    Beans, 75
    in *Greens, Greek*, 117
    in pickled beans, *Dilly Beans*, 75
    in *Pickled Beets*, 159
    in *Salad, Ukrainian Vegetable*, 143
    Sauce, Asparagus with Mustard-, 34
    in *Slaw, Kohlrabi*, 142
    in *Soup with Orzo, Greek Vegetable*, 113
Dipped Strawberries, Chocolate-, 50
Dressing, Cilantro-Lime, 102
dried chiles, 9–10

E

Eastern European seasoning combinations, 24
eggplant
    Armenian Stewed, 81
    grilling/roasting, 20
    Pasta Salad, Roasted, 87
    sauce, *Caponata*, 54
    sautéing, 21
    Stuffed, 78
egg replacement, winter squash pulp as, 15

F

fall dishes/produce, 101
    Acorn Squash and Wild Rice Patties, 126
    Apple Strudel, 149
    Bean and Squash Burgers, 136
    Bell Peppers Stuffed with Black Beans, 139
    Black Bean Chile, 140
    Black Beans, Simple, 130
    Carrots and Jalapeño Chiles, Pickled, 129
    Carrots with Cranberries, Braised, 121

Chard and Chanterelles in Wine Sauce, 119
Chard and Fennel, Pasta with, 132
Chile Paste, Roasted, 106
Cider, Chai Spiced Mulled, 150
Cilantro-Lime Dressing, 102
Collard Greens, Brazilian, 118
Collard Greens, Pasta with, 131
Cranberry Beans, Marinated, 144
Cranberry Beans with Leeks and Fennel, 141
Delicata Succotash, 137
Greens, Greek, 117
Kohlrabi Slaw, 142
Leeks and Chanterelles, Pasta with, 133
Masa Patties with Nuts and Vegetables, 122
Pears, Gingered, 148
Pepperonata, 103
Peppers, Pickled, 128
Pickles, Refrigerator, 145
Pico de Gallo, 106
Potatoes, Twice-Roasted, 116
Pumpkin Seeds, Roasted, 109
Pumpkin Seed Stuffing, 125
Seitan Teriyaki, 135
Soup, Caribbean Pumpkin-Coconut, 112
Soup, Couscous and Roasted Pepper, 114
Soup, French Tomato, 115
Soup, Harvest Corn and Squash, 111
Soup, Parsnip and Fennel, 110
Soup with Orzo, Greek Vegetable, 113
Squash, Parsnip, and Fennel Bruschetta, 107
Squash and Fennel, Lentil Stew with, 138
Squash and Noodle Casserole, 134
Squash Hummus, 102
Squash with Roasted Garlic, Velvety, 120
Tomatillo Salsa, Roasted, 105

Tomato Salsa, Roasted, 104
Vegetable Potato Salad, Mixed, 147
Vegetables, Mexican Roasted, 127
Vegetable Salad, Mexican, 146
Vegetable Salad, Ukrainian, 143
Veggie-Walnut Pinwheels, 108–9
Wild Rice Pilaf, 123
Wild Rice with Cranberries, 124
farmers' markets, 1–2, 4, 5–6, 51, 101, 151
fats, dietary, 21
Fava Beans, Israeli Couscous with Fresh, 90
Fava Beans, Lentil-Barley Salad with Fresh, 89
fennel
    and Arugula Pesto, 56
    Bruschetta, Squash, Parsnip, and, 107
    and Cherry Tomatoes, Purslane with Shaved, 93
    Cranberry Beans with Leeks and, 141
    in *Greek Greens*, 116
    grilling/roasting, 20
    Lentil Stew with Squash and, 138
    Pasta with Chard and, 132
    and Roasted Cherry Tomatoes, Orzo with, 86
    Soup, Parsnip and, 110
    in *Soup, French Tomato*, 115
    and Sweet Peppers, Lentils with, 83
    in *Vegetable Medley, Summer*, 76
fillings/stuffings
    in *Baby Pattypans, Stuffed*, 71
    in *Bell Peppers Stuffed with Black Beans*, 139
    Black Beans, Simple, 130
    in *Cabbage, Summer Stuffed*, 80–81
    in *Cabbage, Winter Stuffed*, 170–71
    Carrots and Jalapeño Chiles, Pickled, 129

in *Eggplant, Stuffed*, 78
in *Grape Leaves, Stuffed*, 84–85
Green Bean-Walnut Pâté, 57
in *Lettuce Rolls, Tofu Stuffed*, 42
Pumpkin Seed Stuffing, 125
Squash Blossoms with Chiles, 61
in *Tomatoes, Pesto Stuffed*, 65
Vegetables, Mexican Roasted, 127
in *Veggie-Walnut Pinwheels*,
    108–9
fingerling potatoes, 14
French Tomato Soup, 115
fresh dishes
    *Fava Beans, Lentil-Barley Salad
        with*, 89
    Mint, Peas and Pea Vines with,
        36
    *Peas, Morel Mushrooms with New
        Potatoes and*, 64
    *Thyme, Roasted Baby Carrots
        with*, 33
Fried Green Tomatoes, 66
Fried Okra, 69

G
garlic, 12, 13
    Beet Greens with Young, 32
    and Herb Sauce, Roasted, 27
    *Sauce, Roasted Brussels Sprouts
        with Lemon-*, 163
    sautéing, 21, 22
    Scapes, White Beans with, 41
    Velvety Squash with Roasted, 120
ginger(ed)
    in *Chai Spiced Mulled Cider*, 150
    Pears, 148
    Sauce, Asparagus with, 35
Glazed Root Vegetables, 164
Gold Beets with Leeks and Chives,
    157
Grape Leaves, Stuffed, 84–85
Gravy, Morel Mushroom, 26
Greek dishes
    orzo used in, 174
    Vegetables, Stewed, 74
    Vegetable Soup with Orzo, 113
Greek seasoning combinations, 24

green bean(s)
    in *Bean Salad, Three*, 94
    with Chickpeas, 77
    Dilly Beans, 75
    *Haricots Verts with Slivered
        Almonds*, 63
    in *Minestrone*, 60
    and New Potato Soup, 59
    in *Succotash, Delicata*, 137
    in *Vegetable Medley, Summer*, 76
    in *Vegetables, Greek Stewed*, 74
    -Walnut Pâté, 57
green bell pepper, in *Salad, Mexican
    Vegetable*, 146
green cabbages, 8
green onions (scallions), 12
greens, 10–11. *See also* specific
    types of
    cooking, 10–11
    Greek, 117
    grilling, advice against, 21
    in *Lentil-Barley Soup*, 152
    in *Scramble, Tofu*, 168
    with Seitan, Mixed, 169
    Squash and, 166
Green Tomatoes, Fried, 66
grilling, 20–21
grits, in *Polenta Primavera*, 44
Gypsy peppers, in *Lentils with
    Fennel and Sweet Peppers*, 83
Gypsy peppers, in *Vegetable Medley,
    Summer*, 76

H
*Haricots Verts with Slivered
    Almonds*, 63
Harvest Corn and Squash Soup, 111
*Hazelnuts, Caramelized Apricots
    with*, 99
Height-of-the-Season Tomato Salad,
    91
heirloom plants, 3
herb(s), 11–12. *See also* specific
    types of
    -Roasted Corn on the Cob, 70
    Sauce, Roasted Garlic and, 27
Homer, 20

hothouse tomatoes, 16
Hubbard squash, 15
Hummus, Squash, 102
hybrid tomatoes, 16

I
Indian seasoning combinations, 24
Irish potato famine, 3
Israeli couscous, 173
*Israeli Couscous with Fresh Fava
    Beans*, 90
Israeli Salad, 91
Italian dishes
    Broccoli Romana, 159
    Green Beans with Chickpeas, 77
    Marsala wine used in, 174
    Minestrone, 60
    Pesto, Sicilian, 55
    pine nuts used in, 174
Italian seasoning combinations, 24

J
jalapeño chiles, 9
*jalapeño Chiles, Pickled Carrots
    and*, 129
Jamaican seasoning combinations,
    24
Japanese dish, *Seitan Teriyaki*, 135
Japanese seasoning combinations,
    24, 135

K
kabocha pumpkin/squash
    in *Soup, Caribbean Pumpkin-
        Coconut*, 112
    in *Soup, Harvest Corn and
        Squash*, 111
    in *Squash and Greens*, 166
kale, 10
    braising, 19
    in *Greens, Squash and*, 166
    in *Greens with Seitan, Mixed*,
        169
    sautéing, 21
    in *Scramble, Tofu*, 168
    *and White Bean Soup,
        Portuguese*, 154

Kappa Maki (Cucumber Sushi Roll), 72
kidney beans, in *Minestrone*, 60
kim chee, 7
Kohlrabi Slaw, 142

L
leek(s), 12, 13
    and Asparagus Curry, 43
    and Carrot Soup, Roasted, 28
    and Chanterelles, Pasta with, 133
    in *Chard and Chanterelles in Wine Sauce*, 119
    and Chives, Gold Beets with, 157
    and Fennel, Cranberry Beans with, 141
    and Parsnip Sauté, 161
    in *Polenta Primavera*, 44
    sautéing, 21
    in *Scramble, Tofu*, 168
    in *Squash and Greens*, 166
    in *Vegetables, Roasted Root*, 165
    in *Wild Rice Pilaf*, 123
Lemon-Garlic Sauce, Roasted Brussels Sprouts with, 163
lentil(s)
    -Barley Salad with Fresh Fava Beans, 89
    -Barley Soup, 152
    in *Curried Vegetable Soup*, 156
    with Fennel and Sweet Peppers, 83
    Soup, Spinach-, 31
    Stew, Yemenite, 79
    Stew with Squash and Fennel, 138
    Tabouli, 88
Lettuce Rolls, Tofu Stuffed, 42
Levi-Strauss, Claude ("The Culinary Triangle"), 19–20
Lime Dressing, Cilantro-, 102
local produce benefits, 2–4

M
manioc flour, 118
Marinated Cranberry Beans, 144
Marsala wine, 174
masa harina, 122, 174

Masa Patties with Nuts and Vegetables, 122
"*Mayonnaise," Panfried Baby Artichokes with Basil*, 68
meat alternative, 135
Medley, Summer Vegetable, 76
Mexican condiment (*Roasted Chile Paste*), 106
Mexican dishes
    Bean and Squash Burgers, 136
    Masa Patties with Nuts and Vegetables, 122
    Vegetables, Roasted, 127
    Vegetable Salad, 146
Mexican dressing, *Cilantro-Lime*, 102
Mexican seasoning combinations, 24
Middle Eastern couscous (Israeli couscous), 173
Middle Eastern dishes
    Chickpea Salad, 88
    Couscous and Roasted Pepper Soup, 114
    Eggplant, Stuffed, 78
    tahini used in, 175
Middle Eastern seasoning combinations, 24
Minestrone, 60
mint, in *Soup with Orzo, Greek Vegetable*, 113
Mint, Peas and Pea Vines with Fresh, 36
Mixed Berry Compote, 98
Mixed Greens with Seitan, 169
Mixed Vegetable Potato Salad, 147
monoculture, 3
Morel Mushroom Gravy, 26
Morel Mushrooms with New Potatoes and Fresh Peas, 64
Mulled Cider, Chai-Spiced, 150
mushroom(s). *See also* specific types of
    Gravy, Morel, 26
    grilling/roasting, 20
    Morel, with New Potatoes and Fresh Peas, 64
    poisonous, 26, 133
    sautéing, 22

    in *Veggie-Walnut Pinwheels*, 108–9
mustard, in *Cabbage-Potato Soup*, 153
Mustard-Dill Sauce, Asparagus with, 34
mustard greens, in *Greens with Seitan, Mixed*, 169
mustard greens, in *Scramble, Tofu*, 168

N
Napa cabbages, 7
Nectarine and Blueberry Cobbler, 100
New Potatoes and Fresh Peas, Morel Mushrooms with, 64
New Potato Soup, Green Bean and, 59
Noodle Casserole, Squash and, 134
nori, 174
North African stew (*Yemenite Lentil Stew*), 79
nutritional yeast flakes (brewer's yeast), 174
nuts. *See also* specific types of
    Persian Radishes and, 48
    and Vegetables, Masa Patties with, 122

O
Okra, Fried, 69
Okra with Tomatoes, 62
olive oil, 21
olive(s)
    Puttanesca Sauce, 53
    in *Salad, Mexican Vegetable*, 146
    in *Sauté, Leek and Parsnip*, 161
omega-3 fatty acids, 21, 93
onion(s), 12–13. *See also* specific types of
    cooking, 13
    grilling/roasting, 20
    sautéing, 21, 22
    in *Vegetable Medley, Summer*, 76
    in *Vegetables, Mexican Roasted*, 127

oregano, fresh, 12
organic food/produce, 3, 4
orzo, 174
*Orzo with Fennel and Roasted
Cherry Tomatoes,* 86

P
*Panfried Baby Artichokes with Basil
"Mayonnaise,"* 68
paprika, 9
Parmentier, 13–14
parsley, 11
parsley, in *Lentil Tabouli,* 88
parsnip(s)
and Fennel Bruschetta, Squash,
107
and Fennel Soup, 110
roasting, 21
Sauté, Leek and, 161
in *Soup, Vegetable-Barley,* 155
in *Vegetables, Glazed Root,* 164
in *Vegetables, Roasted Root,* 165
pasilla chiles, 9
pasta. *See also* pasta sauces
with Chard and Fennel, 132
with Collard Greens, 131
*Couscous and Roasted Pepper
Soup,* 114
*Couscous with Fresh Fava Beans,
Israeli,* 90
with Leeks and Chanterelles, 133
in *Minestrone,* 60
Noodle Casserole, Squash and,
134
orzo, 174
*Orzo, Greek Vegetable Soup
with,* 113
*Orzo with Fennel and Roasted
Cherry Tomatoes,* 86
Salad, Roasted Eggplant, 87
*with Wilted Arugula and Cherry
Tomatoes,* 82
pasta sauces
Caponata, 54
Fennel and Arugula Pesto, 56
Garlic and Herb, Roasted, 27
Pepperonata, 103

Peppers, Pickled, 128
Pesto, Sicilian, 55
Puttanesca, 53
Tomato, Quick, 52
Paste, Roasted Chile, 106
paste, sesame (tahini), 175
Pâté, Green Bean-Walnut, 57
patties
Acorn Squash and Wild Rice, 126
Bean and Squash Burgers, 136
with Nuts and Vegetables, Masa,
122
pattypan squash, 14, 15
Baby, Stuffed, 71
in *Summer Squash with Basil,* 73
Peach-Pecan Cake, 96
Peach Salsa, 58
Peanut Soup, West African, 29
pearl barley, 173
Pears, Gingered, 148
pea(s). *See also* snow peas
*Morel Mushrooms with New
Potatoes and Fresh,* 64
and Pea Vines with Fresh Mint, 36
and Radish Salad, 46
in *Salad, Solstice Steamed
Vegetable,* 47
Pecan Cake, Peach-, 96
peppercorns, in *Chai Spiced Mulled
Cider,* 150
Pepperonata, 103
Peppers, Pickled, 128
Peppers, White Beans with Roasted,
85
*Pepper Soup, Couscous and
Roasted,* 114
Persian Radishes and Nuts, 48
pesticides, 3
pesto
Fennel and Arugula, 56
Sicilian, 55
Stuffed Tomatoes, 65
phyllo dough, in *Apple Strudel,* 149
Piccata, Zucchini, 67
pickles/pickled dishes, 12
Beets, 158
Carrots and Jalapeño Chiles, 129

green beans *(Dilly Beans),* 75
Peppers, 128
Refrigerator, 145
in *Salad, Ukrainian Vegetable,*
143
Sea Beans, 38
Picnic Coleslaw, 92
Pico de Gallo, 106
Pie, Seitan Shepherd's, 167
Pilaf, Wild Rice, 123
pine nuts, 174
Pinwheels, Veggie-Walnut, 108–9
plant food benefits, 2
poblano chiles, 9
Polenta Primavera, 44
polenta sauce, *Caponata,* 54
polenta sauce, *Pepperonata,* 103
*Portuguese Kale and White Bean
Soup,* 154
potato(es), 13–14. *See also* specific
types of
cooking/roasting, 14
grilling/roasting, 20–21
*New, and Fresh Peas, Morel
Mushrooms with,* 64
in *Pie, Seitan Shepherd's,* 167
Salad, Mixed Vegetable, 147
in *Scramble, Tofu,* 168
Soup, Cabbage-, 153
Soup, Green Bean and New, 59
Soup, Puréed Asparagus and, 30
in *Soup, Curried Vegetable,* 156
Twice-Roasted, 116
in *Vegetables, Mexican Roasted,*
127
in *Vegetables, Roasted Root,*
165
Primavera, Polenta, 44
pumpkin(s), 15
-Coconut Soup, Caribbean, 112
Seeds, Roasted, 109
Seed Stuffing, 125
Puréed Asparagus and Potato Soup,
30
purple pole beans, in *Three Bean
Salad,* 94
purple potatoes, 14

Purslane with Shaved Fennel and
    Cherry Tomatoes, 93
Puttanesca Sauce, 53

Q

Quick Tomato Sauce, 52
quinoa, 174

R

Radishes and Nuts, Persian, 48
Radish Salad, Pea and, 46
raspberries, in Mixed Berry
    Compote, 98
Raspberry-Almond Cake, 97
red ancho chiles, 10
red bell pepper(s)
    in Pepper Soup, Couscous and
        Roasted, 114
    in Polenta Primavera, 44
    in Seitan Teriyaki, 135
red cabbages, 8
red onion, in Picnic Coleslaw, 92
red potato, in Vegetable-Barley
    Soup, 155
Refrigerator Pickles, 145
regeneration, 3
relish dish, Pickled Carrots and
    Jalapeño Chiles, 129
relish dish, Pickled Peppers, 128
Rhubarb Tart, Strawberry-, 49
Rice Patties, Acorn Squash and
    Wild, 126
Rice Pilaf, Wild, 123
Rice with Cranberries, Wild, 124
roasted dishes/roasting, 19–21
    Baby Carrots with Fresh Thyme,
        33
    Brussels Sprouts with Lemon-
        Garlic Sauce, 163
    Chile Paste, 106
    chiles, 9
    Corn on the Cob, Herb-, 70
    delicata squash, 15
    Eggplant Pasta Salad, 87
    Garlic, Velvety Squash with, 120
    Garlic and Herb Sauce, 27
    Leek and Carrot Soup, 28

Peppers, White Beans with, 85
Pepper Soup, Couscous and, 114
potatoes, 14
Potatoes, Twice-, 116
Pumpkin Seeds, 109
Root Vegetables, 165
seeds, winter squash, 15
Tomatillo Salsa, 105
tomatoes, 17
Tomato Salsa, 104
Vegetables, Mexican, 127
winter squash, 15, 16
Roll, Cucumber Sushi (Kappa
    Maki), 72
Rolls, Tofu Stuffed Lettuce, 42
Romana, Broccoli, 159
Roma tomatoes, 16
root vegetables, 151. See also spe-
    cific types of
    braising, 19
    Glazed, 164
    Roasted, 165
rosemary, fresh, 12
russet potatoes, 14

S

Safeway, 4
salad(s)
    addition to, Balsamic Cipollini
        Onions, 73
    addition to, Marinated Cranberry
        Beans, 144
    Beet and Walnut, 171
    Chickpea, Middle Eastern, 88
    Coleslaw, Picnic, 92
    Cucumber, Curried, 93
    Dressing, Cilantro-Lime, 102
    Eggplant Pasta, Roasted, 87
    Israeli, 91
    Lentil-Barley, with Fresh Fava
        Beans, 89
    Lentil Tabouli, 88
    Pea and Radish, 46
    Persian Radishes and Nuts, 48
    Purslane with Shaved Fennel and
        Cherry Tomatoes, 93
    Slaw, Kohlrabi, 142

Three Bean, 94
tomato, 17, 91
Tomato, Height-of-the-Season, 91
topping, Pickled Peppers, 128
Vegetable, Mexican, 146
Vegetable, Solstice Steamed, 47
Vegetable, Ukrainian, 143
Vegetable Potato, Mixed, 147
salsa(s)
    Peach, 58
    Pico de Gallo, 106
    Roasted Tomatillo, 105
    Roasted Tomato, 104
sauce(s)
    Caponata, 54
    Garlic and Herb, Roasted, 27
    Ginger, Asparagus with, 35
    Lemon-Garlic, Roasted Brussels
        Sprouts with, 163
    Mustard-Dill, Asparagus with, 34
    Pepperonata, 103
    Pesto, Fennel and Arugula, 56
    Pesto, Sicilian, 55
    Puttanesca, 53
    Tomato, Quick, 52
    Wine, Chard and Chanterelles in,
        119
sauerkraut, 7
Sauté, Leek and Parsnip, 161
sautéing, 19, 21–22
Savoy cabbages, 8
Savoy Cabbage with Cashews, 162
scallions (green onions), 12
Scapes, White Beans with Garlic, 41
Scramble, Tofu, 168
Sea Beans, Pickled, 38
seasonings, 23–24
Seattle farmers' markets, 1–2
sea vegetable (nori), 174
seeds, 3. See also specific types of
seitan, 135, 174–75
    Mixed Greens with, 169
    Shepherd's Pie, 167
    Teriyaki, 135
sesame paste (tahini), 175
Sesame Snow Peas, 39
shallots, 12, 13

in *Chard and Chanterelles in Wine Sauce*, 119
sautéing, 21
in *Squash and Greens*, 166
in *Veggie-Walnut Pinwheels*, 108–9
in *Wild Rice Pilaf*, 123
Shaved Fennel and Cherry Tomatoes, Purslane with, 93
Shepherd's Pie, Seitan, 167
Sicilian Pesto, 55
Simple Black Beans, 130
simplicity, in cooking, 5–6
Slaw, Kohlrabi, 142
Slivered Almonds, Haricots Verts with, 63
snack, *Roasted Pumpkin Seeds*, 109
snack, *Veggie-Walnut Pinwheels*, 108–9
snow peas, in *Solstice Steamed Vegetable Salad*, 47
Snow Peas, Sesame, 39
Solstice Steamed Vegetable Salad, 47
Sorrel with Spring Onions, 37
soup(s)
    Asparagus and Potato, Puréed, 30
    Corn and Squash, Harvest, 111
    Couscous and Roasted Pepper, 114
    Green Bean and New Potato, 59
    Kale and White Bean, Portuguese, 154
    Leek and Carrot, Roasted, 28
    Lentil-Barley, 152
    Minestrone, 60
    with *Orzo, Greek Vegetable*, 113
    Parsnip and Fennel, 110
    Peanut, West African, 29
    Spinach-Lentil, 31
    thickeners in, 14, 16
    Tomato, French, 115
    Vegetable, Curried, 156
    Vegetable-Barley, 155
Southern dishes
    corn grits used in, 173
    Okra, Fried, 69
    Peach-Pecan Cake, 96

Tomatoes, Fried Green, 66
spaghetti squash, 15, 16
Spiced Mulled Cider, Chai, 150
spices, 11
spinach
    Afghani, 40
    in *Greens, Greek*, 117
    in *Greens, Squash and*, 166
    -*Lentil Soup*, 31
    sautéing, 21–22
    in *Scramble, Tofu*, 168
    in *Soup, Lentil-Barley*, 152
spring dishes/produce, 25
    Asparagus with Ginger Sauce, 35
    Asparagus with Mustard-Dill Sauce, 34
    Baby Bok Choy with Tofu, 45
    Baby Carrots with Fresh Thyme, Roasted, 33
    Beet Greens with Young Garlic, 32
    Garlic and Herb Sauce, Roasted, 27
    Leek and Asparagus Curry, 43
    Lettuce Rolls, Tofu Stuffed, 42
    Morel Mushroom Gravy, 26
    Peas and Pea Vines with Fresh Mint, 36
    Polenta Primavera, 44
    Salad, Pea and Radish, 46
    Salad, Persian Radishes and Nuts, 48
    Salad, Solstice Steamed Vegetable, 47
    Sea Beans, Pickled, 38
    Snow Peas, Sesame, 39
    Sorrel with Spring Onions, 37
    Soup, Puréed Asparagus and Potato, 30
    Soup, Roasted Leek and Carrot, 28
    Soup, Spinach-Lentil, 31
    Soup, West African Peanut, 29
    Spinach, Afghani, 40
    Strawberries, Chocolate-Dipped, 50
    Strawberry-Rhubarb Tart, 49

White Beans with Garlic Scapes, 41
Spring Onions, Sorrel with, 37
squash, 14–16. *See also* specific types of
    Burgers, Bean and, 136
    cooking, 15–16
    and Fennel, Lentil Stew with, 138
    and Greens, 166
    Hummus, 102
    and Noodle Casserole, 134
    Parsnip, and Fennel Bruschetta, 107
    pulp, as egg replacement, 15
    with Roasted Garlic, Velvety, 120
    Soup, Harvest Corn and, 111
    in soups, as thickener, 16
squash blossoms, 15
Squash Blossoms with Chiles, 61
Steamed Vegetable Salad, Solstice, 47
steaming, 19, 22
stew/stewed dishes/stewing, 19
    Eggplant, Armenian, 81
    Lentil, with Squash and Fennel, 138
    Lentil, Yemenite, 79
    Vegetables, Greek, 74
stir-fry, pea vines in, 36
stir-frying, vs. sautéing, 21
strawberry(ies)
    in *Berry Compote, Mixed*, 98
    Chocolate-Dipped, 50
    -*Rhubarb Tart*, 49
Strudel, Apple, 149
stuffed dishes
    Baby Pattypans, 71
    Bell Peppers Stuffed with Black Beans, 139
    Cabbage, Summer, 80–81
    Cabbage, Winter, 170–71
    Eggplant, 78
    Grape Leaves, 84–85
    Lettuce Rolls, Tofu, 42
    Tomatoes, Pesto, 65
Succotash, Delicata, 137
summer dishes/produce, 51
    Apricots with Hazelnuts, Caramelized, 99

Arugula and Cherry Tomatoes, Pasta with Wilted, 82
Baby Artichokes with Basil "Mayonnaise," Panfried, 68
Baby Pattypans, Stuffed, 71
Beans, Dilly, 75
Berry Compote, Mixed, 98
Blueberry Bars, 95
Cabbage, Summer Stuffed, 80–81
Caponata, 54
Cipollini Onions, Balsamic, 73
Corn on the Cob, Herb-Roasted, 70
Eggplant, Stuffed, 78
Fava Beans, Israeli Couscous with Fresh, 90
Fennel and Arugula Pesto, 56
Fennel and Roasted Cherry Tomatoes, Orzo with, 86
Grape Leaves, Stuffed, 84–85
Green Bean and New Potato Soup, 59
Green Beans with Chickpeas, 77
Green Bean-Walnut Pâté, 57
Haricots Verts with Slivered Almonds, 63
Kappa Maki (Cucumber Sushi Roll), 72
Lentil Stew, Yemenite, 79
Lentils with Fennel and Sweet Peppers, 83
Minestrone, 60
Morel Mushrooms with New Potatoes and Fresh Peas, 64
Nectarine and Blueberry Cobbler, 100
Okra, Fried, 69
Okra with Tomatoes, 62
Peach-Pecan Cake, 96
Peach Salsa, 58
Pesto, Sicilian, 55
Puttanesca Sauce, 53
Raspberry-Almond Cake, 97
Salad, Curried Cucumber, 93
Salad, Height-of-the-Season Tomato, 91
Salad, Israeli, 91

salad, Lentil Tabouli, 88
Salad, Middle Eastern Chickpea, 88
salad, Picnic Coleslaw, 92
salad, Purslane with Shaved Fennel and Cherry Tomatoes, 93
Salad, Roasted Eggplant Pasta, 87
Salad, Three Bean, 94
Salad with Fresh Fava Beans, Lentil-Barley, 89
Squash Blossoms with Chiles, 61
Summer Squash with Basil, 73
Tomatoes, Fried Green, 66
Tomatoes, Pesto Stuffed, 65
Tomato Sauce, Quick, 52
Vegetable Medley, Summer, 76
Vegetables, Greek Stewed, 74
White Beans with Roasted Peppers, 85
Zucchini Piccata, 67
summer squash, 14, 15
with Basil, 73
sautéing, 22
sunburst squash, 15
Sun Gold tomatoes, 16
Sushi Roll, Cucumber (Kappa Maki), 72
sweet-and-sour dish, Lentils with Fennel and Sweet Peppers, 83
Sweet Peppers, Lentils with Fennel and, 83

T

Tabouli, Lentil, 88
tahini, 175
Tart, Strawberry-Rhubarb, 49
Teriyaki, Seitan, 135
Thai basil, 11
Thai chiles, 9
Thai seasoning combinations, 24
"The Culinary Triangle" (Levi-Strauss), 19
Third World countries, 3
Three Bean Salad, 94
thyme, 12

Thyme, Roasted Baby Carrots with Fresh, 33
tofu (bean curd), 175
Baby Bok Choy with, 45
in Casserole, Squash and Noodle, 134
in Coleslaw, Picnic, 92
Scramble, 168
in Slaw, Kohlrabi, 142
Stuffed Lettuce Rolls, 42
Tomatillo Salsa, Roasted, 105
tomato(es), 16–17. See also cherry tomatoes
bruised, 16–17
cooking, 17
Fried Green, 66
in Minestrone, 60
Okra with, 62
in Pepperonata, 103
Pesto Stuffed, 65
in Pico de Gallo, 106
Salad, Height-of-the-Season, 91
in Salad, Israeli, 91
in Salad, Mexican Vegetable, 146
in Salad, Middle Eastern Chickpea, 88
in Salad, Three Bean, 94
Salsa, Roasted, 104
Sauce, Quick, 52
in sautéing, 21
Soup, French, 115
in Soup, Harvest Corn and Squash, 111
in Soup with Orzo, Greek Vegetable, 113
in Stewed Eggplant, Armenian, 81
in Stewed Vegetables, Greek, 74
in Stew with Squash and Fennel, Lentil, 138
in Stuffed Cabbage, Summer, 80–81
in Succotash, Delicata, 137
in Tabouli, Lentil, 88
trans fats, 21
turnips
Braised, 160
roasting, 21

sautéing, 21
in *Vegetables, Glazed Root,* 164
in *Vegetables, Roasted Root,* 165
Twice-Roasted Potatoes, 116

U

Ukrainian Vegetable Salad, 143

V

vegan Worcestershire sauce, 175
vegetable(s). *See also* specific types of
-Barley Soup, 155
Greek Stewed, 74
Masa Patties with Nuts and, 122
Medley, Summer, 76
Mexican Roasted, 127
Pinwheels, Veggie-Walnut, 108–9
Potato Salad, Mixed, 147
Salad, Mexican, 146
Salad, Solstice Steamed, 47
Salad, Ukrainian, 143
Soup, Curried, 156
soup *(Minestrone),* 60
Soup with Orzo, Greek, 113
Velvety Squash with Roasted Garlic,
120

W

Wal-Mart, 4
walnut
Pâté, Green Bean-, 57
Pinwheels, Veggie-, 108–9
Salad, Beet and, 171
Waters, Alice, 5
West African Peanut Soup, 29
white bean(s)
with Garlic Scapes, 41
with Roasted Peppers, 85

Soup, Portuguese Kale and, 154
in *Succotash, Delicata,* 137
white cabbages, 8
white potatoes, in *Seitan Shepherd's
Pie,* 167
wild rice
with Cranberries, 124
Patties, Acorn Squash and, 126
Pilaf, 123
*Wilted Arugula and Cherry
Tomatoes, Pasta with,* 82
*Wine Sauce, Chard and Chanterelles
in,* 119
winter dishes/produce, 151
Apple Crisp, 172
Beet and Walnut Salad, 171
Beets, Pickled, 158
Broccoli Romana, 159
*Brussels Sprouts with Lemon-
Garlic Sauce, Roasted,* 163
Cabbage, Winter Stuffed, 170–71
*Gold Beets with Leeks and
Chives,* 157
Greens with Seitan, Mixed, 169
Leek and Parsnip Sauté, 161
Root Vegetables, Glazed, 164
Root Vegetables, Roasted, 165
Savoy Cabbage with Cashews,
162
Scramble, Tofu, 168
Seitan Shepherd's Pie, 167
Soup, Cabbage-Potato, 153
Soup, Curried Vegetable, 156
Soup, Lentil-Barley, 152
*Soup, Portuguese Kale and White
Bean,* 154
Soup, Vegetable-Barley, 155
Squash and Greens, 166

Turnips, Braised, 160
winter squash, 14–15
roasting, 21
in *Soup, Caribbean Pumpkin-
Coconut,* 112
in *Squash and Greens,* 166
winter vegetables, 12
Worcestershire sauce, vegan, 175

Y

yams, in *Veggie-Walnut Pinwheels,*
108–9
yams, roasting, 21
yellow beets, in *Glazed Root
Vegetables,* 164
yellow crookneck squash, 14
yellow crookneck squash, in
Summer Squash with Basil, 73
yellow wax beans, in *Three Bean
Salad,* 94
Yeminite Lentil Stew, 79
Young Garlic, Beet Greens with, 32
Yukon Gold potato(es), 14
in *Potatoes, Twice-Roasted,* 116
in *Soup, Vegetable-Barley,* 155

Z

zucchini, 14
grilling/roasting, 20
Piccata, 67
in *Salad, Mexican Vegetable,* 146
in *Seitan Teriyaki,* 135
in *Summer Squash with Basil,* 73
in *Vegetables, Greek Stewed,* 74
in *Vegetables, Masa Patties with
Nuts and,* 122
in *Vegetables, Mexican Roasted,*
127

BOOK PUBLISHING COMPANY

since 1974—books that educate, inspire, and empower

To find your favorite vegetarian and alternative health books online, visit:

www.healthy-eating.com

Omega 3 Cuisine

Alan Roettinger

978-0-920470-81-7 • $19.95

Intuitive Cooking

Joanne Saltzman

978-1-57067-194-4 • $19.95

  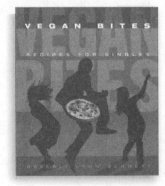

*The Ultimate
Uncheese Cookbook*

Jo Stepaniak

978-1-57067-151-7 • $18.95

Organic Pest Control

Tom Roberts

978-1-57067-052-7

$12.95

Vegan Bites

Beverly Lynn Bennett

978-1-57067-221-7

$14.95

Purchase these health titles and cookbooks from your local bookstore
or natural food store, or you can buy them directly from:

Book Publishing Company • P.O. Box 99 • Summertown, TN 38483
1-800-695-2241

Please include $3.95 per book for shipping and handling.